ROBERT R HOLMES

ONE FISH

CHANGES EVERYTHING

Leadership Lessons Learned
The Most Unexpected Way

Special thanks to all of those who supported me by listening as I read through sections of my project with them or taking the time to read my manuscript in raw form. I couldn't have completed this without the confidence provided from your feedback: Tracy Sears, Mark Rigsby, Mike Brubaker, Jennifer Holmes, Dave Jansen, Michele Kelly, Brittany Raschdorf, Ruth Morris, Katie Bischoff, John Castelino, Todd Hoffman, Jackie Camacho-Ruiz, Doug Garasic, Dena Massaro-Williams, Michael Wahl, Greg Preston, and Harrison Rogers. You all are the best!!!

For information contact:
info@onefishchanges.com
Website: http://www.onefishchanges.com
Facebook: http://www.facebook.com/onefishchanges
Twitter: https://twitter.com/onefishchanges
Instagram: https://www.instagram.com/onefishchanges/

Cover design by Robert Holmes
This cover and book has been designed using resources from Freepik

ISBN: 978-1-7342369-4-1
Library of Congress Control Number: 2019920472

First Edition: December 2019

DEDICATION

"Just remember, Bobby, you can do anything you want to do and be anything you want to be. Never forget that. Don't let anyone ever tell you that you can't."

I heard these simple words of encouragement over and over as a young boy. This book I dedicate to my Mom, Doris Holmes. "Dodie," as she was called by her friends, was the most influential, loving, caring, and compassionate person in my life. From patiently sitting with me and encouraging me to perfect my sketching, to inspiring me as I chased after my musical dreams, my car building dreams, my dreams to be an entrepreneur and any other thing I set my eyes upon, "You can do anything" still resonates in my ears today. This world lost an amazing person in July of 2018 and Heaven gained a new angel. I dedicate this book to my Mom for always believing in me and loving me unconditionally.

For every mentor or friend who has taken time to invest in the well-being of others. **Here's to you!**

ACKNOWLEDGMENTS

Special thanks to the many fishing partners I have been blessed to share time on the water with. Starting with the late John P. Schaffer who, as the Mayor of my hometown, genuinely invested in me as a teenage boy by asking his young neighbor to be his fishing partner. Boy did we catch 'em.

Thanks to the late Brian Spackman for the willingness to walk four miles with waders and work hard all day long on Saturday morning. We will fish together in Heaven one day and you will get another shot at that giant northern you hooked on a Marabou jig and fought for what seemed like hours before it cut the line.

Thanks to John DeFalco for inviting me to ride in the back of a pick-up truck to Northern Ontario where we landed 528 northern pike in one week.

Thanks to Darrin Littleton for helping me carry the boat to Mosquito Creek hundreds of times and many nights on the shore.

Thanks to Scotty "Whapper" Spetsios for many days and nights with tight lines.

Thanks to Greg Preston for always being up for getting on a dock or pond on a short notice (Whoever stole his flat bottom boat from behind our office– shame on you!).

Thanks to Gregg Sprinkel for finding out what happens to a school of hybrid bass when a high-pressure system finally releases.

Thanks to Jeff "Big Fish" Castleberry who wasn't shy about inviting this Yankee to fish with him and Jeff "King Fish" Hertling for doubling our chances of success.

Thanks to Jim Moudry for always reminding me he caught more than me once. We could hardly lift the stringer.

Thanks to Randy Hepworth who is the master of the gulf, first class person and a mentor.

Thanks for the incredible southern hospitality. My amazing family, Jen, Gavin, and Rylan for agreeing that no matter where we travel on vacation, we will find someplace to fish (beginning with our honeymoon).

Also, thanks to the many people who have casted lines alongside me. You know who you are. Sometimes we caught them and sometimes we didn't, but we ALWAYS influenced each other in one way or another.

Also, thanks to the leaders that have helped form my perspective: Larry Harper, Jim Mahan, Bill Flaherty, Marcus Graham, Ernie Zavoral, Tommy Willingham, Frank Bernat, Jody Webb, Michael Wahl, Dave Jansen and of course my Dad, Robert J. Holmes…Thank You.

Special thanks to Craig Fauvie for saving my life in 1996. The greatest perspective change of all.

C O N T E N T S

INTRODUCTION

The world is moving fast, and, in many cases, it feels like our society is moving in the wrong direction. More than anything, we are disconnecting from relationships and connecting with our phones, our technology or, often times, consuming ourselves with self-pity. If you study broken lives and broken people, many have spent a lifetime overcoming their insecurity and their lack of confidence. One way we try to compensate is by pouring ourselves into something we are confident in and working hard to develop the skills to win. That could be business, sports, art, or so many different things. These activities become all-consuming and require so much dedicated passion and selfish focus.

So, what suffers? Typically, our relationships with one another suffer and we can't live up to our own expectations, because we can't always win or be on top (as much as we would all love to).

What helps? Often, real relationships, mentors, helping others and a realization of the fact that we are not in total control. These are things that help change our mindset.

Do you see the problem? Our relationships suffer but real relationships are a part of the cure. We think it all depends on us and that pressure adds up.

How many people do you walk by every day that you cordially address, but you really know nothing about them? Do you remain consumed by your own thoughts? Do you let your surroundings determine your well-being? I wrote the main character "Bags" to carry the characteristics of someone who is always down on himself, ignoring his neighbor, hard to deal with, has very few friends. After some bad decisions and unfortunate luck, he is not moving forward in life and, quite frankly, isn't trying. The only thing he is passionate about is fishing. Oddly enough, a series of events leads him to uncover that an unlikely character can be his best chance of landing a giant. He sets out on a journey that enables him to grasp a simple four-step approach to reaching his goals. He learns clear lessons of communicating with confidence, realizes patience is a part of every strategic plan, soaks up the importance of perspective, and recognizes that no matter how well you strategize you are never in complete control. Most important he realizes that one fish changes everything!

Take these principles to heart. We all need relationship with others to sharpen us. We also need to understand it will not always turn out the way we expect. We should always prepare and plan to the best of abilities, but we should be okay if it doesn't work out the way we planned. The old priest enables Bags to see this when sharing his religious beliefs, but no matter what your beliefs, these principles are sound. They will enable you to be okay not catching the biggest fish in the lake, and much more thankful if you do.

Thanks for reading, and please strive to pour yourself into others...share you! It helps us all!

Robert Holmes

FOREWORDS

BY TODD HOFFMAN

When Robert reached out to me, we hadn't talked for a few years. But shortly into the conversation, I felt compelled to tell him about some of the great things my dad Jack and I have been doing. I told him about the drug and alcohol recovery center we recently started and shared with him the story of a young girl who graduated in the latest class. Although we hadn't talked in a few years, this is the kind of conversation that always seems to happen with Robert. In fact, he said, "Todd, this is exactly why I thought of you to write the foreword for my book. All this TV stuff and gold mining you do is cool, but when it comes down to it, it is those kinds of moments that really count, and you get it."

I have to admit that I wasn't super excited about writing this. In fact, I challenged Robert on the whole idea of a book. I warned him that books are hard to sell. He was passionate about why he wrote the book and felt like there was something bigger happening here that he couldn't explain. I was still reluctant but agreed to read his manuscript. At one point in our conversation, Robert said to me the book is just a part of a bigger plan and the plan isn't mine. I could understand that and agreed to give it a shot.

What I didn't expect was a story with such emotion and character development. Although, it makes sense to me now because of the level of interaction I have seen from Robert with the people around him. You can tell he pays close attention to people and that comes across in this book. The story has some real nuggets of wisdom that stick with you long after you read it. There have been plenty of times in my life that I could have used those nuggets. Whether it's a lesson about preparation, planning, relationships or the need to invest in others, there are many takeaways in this book. As I said earlier, in regard to the important things in life, Robert said to me, "you get it." Based on the interactions between the main characters in this book, he obviously gets it too.

Those who know me know that I am anything but perfect, but I am not afraid to share my faith. In the book, I found it intriguing how Father DeFalco never pressures Bags but openly shares when asked. In fact, he found a way to edge him ever closer to understanding without doing anything but speaking truth and simply referring to how to handle yourself in life. Of course, he thought the old man was teaching him how to fish, but he was making a difference in the way he saw the world and others around him.

So, when I finally acquiesced to reading the manuscript, I should have known that it would move me, and it did. I am thankful that Robert asked me to take part in this journey with him and I wish him all the luck in his future endeavors. I hope you take away as much as I did and if you are reluctant, it may mean something special is about to happen. Good luck!

Todd Hoffman

Gold Miner, TV Personality, Humanitarian

BY GREG PRESTON (FISHING PARTNER)

When my good friend, Robert, told me that he had written a book, I was not shocked. In our twenty-plus years of friendship, I have known him to be a man of many talents. So again, I was not shocked. But I was surprised; surprised that he had the time to write a book.

Robert Holmes is a person that never does anything halfway. He is a man of passion who pours his heart, time, and energy into everything he does. And when he commits himself to something, you can guarantee that it will be a success. After reading his first book, I have no doubt that One Fish Changes Everything will also fall into the category of successful.

Robert has always been a marketing whiz, propelling companies forward, growing their name recognition and revenues through his well-calculated and creative approach. In addition to the demanding jobs he has held over the years, he always had a successful side business or two as well. Not just in his field of marketing, but varied businesses built on some of his other passions, like food and religion. We are talking about a person whose parents had to install a second phone line when Robert was young because his business was consuming the family's only phone line.

Robert and I went to work for the same dynamic company over 20 years ago. We immediately became friends and shortly thereafter became the best of fishing buddies. We fished freshwater and saltwater, crappie and stripers, winter and summer. It didn't matter as long as we were on the water with a line in the water. And, although we were usually lucky enough to catch fish, it didn't matter as long as we were learning from each other about fishing and life.

I said that we were "lucky enough" to catch fish. As I was reading *One Fish Changes Everything*, it dawned on me that it wasn't just luck. Robert always had a well laid-out plan, using the same fundamental principles he lays out in this book. Principles that can apply to everyday life and help each and every one of us be the best that we can be.

With all of Robert's business success, one might think that he is one of these people driven by money and material wealth. Nothing could be further from the truth. His greatest passion is people. Robert loves people. He pours himself into his businesses, but always finds time for helping others. His dedication to his church, family, and his friends is constant and consistent. I recall one example of his love for people when Robert took in a young man for over a year, provided him a warm bed and mentoring, changing the young man's life.

One Fish Changes Everything is not necessarily about fishing. It is a self-help book disguised as an engaging, fast-moving story about Joey, who is nicknamed Bags, and his love for fishing. I loved the adventure of Bags and the lessons I learned along the way. Let's hope that this is not Robert Holmes' "last cast."

Greg Preston
Strategic Sales Professional, Fishing Partner

CHAPTER ONE

PIZZA, PASSION & THE PRIEST

It was 5:30 a.m. on a beautiful winter morning. It was the time of the year when I was longing for sunshine, I was longing for smiles, and I was longing for positive energy to help with my well-being. That particular morning, I really longed for more sleep. Just another fifteen minutes? Do I have to be there by eight o'clock? Can I be a little late this morning? Will anyone notice? These are some of the questions I asked myself as I got ready to leave my house. Why did I seem to struggle this time of year? No matter what kind of happy little tune I put in my alarm clock, my mind converted the sound to something negative, and my body responded by not wanting to move. My mind took these major-scaled, happy little melodies and turned them into disturbing and distorted minor progressions that seemed a little evil. The song I woke up to seemed to somehow ask me, dauntingly, if I was ready for the day. Some mornings I was motivated by the sounds in my head, and I arose searching for victory. That morning I was feeling defeated. I felt as if the minor chords I heard spelled doom. I was not excited about putting my feet on the ground. Of course I would, and I did.

That morning was not unlike most other Mondays. It was February 28 in Northeast Ohio, where snow had covered the remnants of the steel factories for what seemed like a lifetime. We had experienced a healthy dose of lake effect snow that year. Temperatures were consistently cold and snowfall on top of snowfall had kept most of us Midwesterners to ourselves far more than the average winter.

When we were young, the snow would draw us out of

our homes to enjoy the winter fun. Many years ago, when the economy was strong, people were active, and the parks were full of sledders and skaters. These days, most people just chose to stay inside and rely on the six o'clock newscast to learn about what's happening outside. The parks no longer filled the skating rinks with water because of budget cuts. The sledding hills that used to be active were blocked off with barricades out of fear that someone would get hurt and the park would be dropped by the insurance company. Somehow, we accepted this as okay. In fact, we accepted this as necessary. After all, our six o'clock connection with our favorite newscasters showed us that we risked murder, car accidents, unemployment, disease, or mistreatment of some other type if we made the asserted effort to leave our homes. So we just chose to stay inside, questioned why we ever elected to live in that God-forsaken place, and continued to believe that one day it would get better. We just continued to trust that some political leader would eliminate the organized crime, bring jobs back to our small towns and, ultimately, shorten our winters. Or... at least our perception of them.

That next day was the beginning of March and I knew spring was not far away, even though the weatherman said we were going to get another two to four inches of snow with a high temperature of eight degrees. I was reading about tactics for spring fishing on lakes Mosquito, Milton and Pymatuning, although, I could have driven a truck across any of those lakes without any hesitation at the time. My inner being longed to throw my flat bottom boat in the back of my friend Scott's truck. That way, I could forget about my friends on the six o'clock newscast and spend some time challenging myself to put fish in the boat. Now, I am thirty-seven years old and I still dream of holding a lake record on any of those bodies of water. In fact, that dream has been in me for so long that it borders on obsession. Same pattern every year. Same timeline. Same dreaming before ice-off and same old longing for new equipment, new electronics and any other means of getting an advantage on the elusive, freshwater giants.

I work at the local pizza restaurant, Prezioso Pizza and Pasta where I spend Mondays prep-cooking for the week. I pretty much do everything around the restaurant and Johnny, whose family has owned the restaurant for over seventy years, has been good to me. He pays me cash under the table every week so I can still get my disability pay and no one questions it. You probably wonder what disability I have, and I can tell you that some disabilities run much deeper than a physical limitation. It happened about ten years ago when I was struggling to find a job after the local auto manufacturer laid off a couple thousand people. I happened to be a part of that illustrious group. I have no other way to explain it other than just telling you the simple truth. I had a meltdown. I lost it and tried to take my own life. There I was, a young man still in his twenties, in fairly good shape, with a master's degree from Cleveland State in Business Administration and good operations and supply chain experience, and not a single opportunity in over a year. I loved my job and I was good at it. My reviews were always positive and I was told by many of our leaders that I had a long career ahead of me. Then, just like that, I was looking for a job again.

I had a few opportunities down south, but this is my home. I couldn't imagine leaving my friends and family and starting over somewhere else. Then my counselor let me know I could apply for disability, receive a check from the government every month, and not really have to be concerned with finding a job. So that is exactly what I did.

Some of my friends said I was crazy for not exploring those opportunities down south, but I saw the best of our high school class move away, only to be back a few years later. My good friend Scott, who happens to share my obsession for lake records, moved away for almost fifteen years before returning home. I started to think he wasn't coming back but inside I knew better. It was only a matter of time. He moved back here about five years ago and we have been sharing fishing tactics and driving friendly competitions ever since. Sometimes Scott drives the boat and sometimes I take the helm. Either way we put in our best effort to get the biggest possible fish in the boat. Sometimes we are successful at landing some really nice fish and sometimes we are successful at sharing life's challenges, as I often need his encouragement. We haven't spoke much this winter, but I am sure he is thinking the same things I am right about now. Scott got married in the fall, but he assured me it wouldn't change anything, and we would still get on the lake right after ice-off. I know I keep talking about fishing but like I said earlier, it is almost an obsession.

On my way to work, I noticed how cold it was. I wasn't sure what the temperature was outside, but by how quickly my nose hair froze when I cleaned the snow off of my car, I was willing to bet it was something below zero. I scrape the ice off my windows because I have no garage to park my car in at the duplex I am currently renting. I had moved into this place November of last year and I'll be honest, I have seen my neighbors from a distance, and I hear them every time they flush the toilet, but I have not spoken to them. I have seen a woman who looks like she's in her mid to late twenties and has a couple of kids maybe six or seven years old. I am really bad at guessing the age of children, but I can guess the weight of a bigmouth bass within a few ounces. Once again, I show signs of obsession, or maybe just a lack of concern about relationships with other humans.

I was almost to Prezioso Pizza and Pasta that morning and my car had just started to warm up. I drive a 1986 Oldsmobile Cutlass that Johnny lets me make weekly payments on. He takes it straight from my pay and doesn't charge me much. It isn't a bad car, it's just old. It smells old, like a mix of oil and anti-freeze. Most people look at my car and are surprised it still runs. The wide chrome strip down the passenger side nearly falls off every time I shut the door because the clips are rusted off. Nevertheless, it gets me to where I need to go, and I had the honor of making the famous Prezioso red sauce to top the pizza and pasta, and my Cutlass got me there with plenty of time to spare. Fifteen minutes to be exact. I pulled up to the back doors at exactly 7:45 and I couldn't wait to see if someone had made coffee yet. It was far too cold to stay in my car, and I needed to be warmed up from the inside out.

Oh yeah... I have just been rambling and forgot to introduce myself. My name is Joey Alfieri and my friends call me "Bags." They call me this because I am known for carrying around a lot of baggage. I guess I not only carry it around, but I must be more open about it than the average person. I must talk about my problems a lot for a name like that to stick with me all these years. Nearly everyone in this small town calls me Bags, and I think it all started after I lost my parents in my early twenties. They both passed away in a bad car accident on the way home from the high school football game less than a mile from our house. It was a trying time from my family. Most of my uncles and aunts were never the same. As a single child, I moved in with my grandfather and focused on finishing college. My grandpa did the best he could to help me through it all. I kind of remember being at a party and my friends called me out for always being a downer and I think it was my buddy Jeff who first called me Bags and it stuck. None-the-less, during this time our whole town really rallied around my family. My hometown is nicknamed little Italy so most of my friends' family names end in an I or an O, like mine and I think that is a part of the reason everyone sticks together. It is the culture.

As I pulled up to the pizza shop that morning, I saw some of Prezioso's finest young men standing in the back of the restaurant enjoying a smoke. I said enjoying, but I wasn't sure how that was even possible when it was so cold it hurt to breathe. You had to question the sanity of those three young, fourth generation Italian boys. Jimmy, Nick, and Tino were their names and they didn't have a worry in the world. They graduated high school together and all chose not to go to college. They were there every Monday morning ready to cut vegetables for primavera, can hot peppers in oil for the week, and cut up onions and peppers for the famous Prezioso Italian hot sausage and peppers.

As I got out of my Cutlass, they started right away with, "It's Monday morning and Bags is here to make the sauce. Ain't that right Bags?" I replied, like clockwork, "You bet-ya boys, I am here to make the best red sauce in the county, the country, maybe the world. Admit it boys, that's what keeps you coming back. The dream of one day making the sauce. Maybe one day boys, maybe one day." I slammed my car door and it didn't quite shut all the way because it needed a new door pin and it had been too dang cold to fix it. I had the part I just didn't want to freeze my hands off changing it out. Plus, I needed an extra hand to hold the door and extra hands were hard to find this time of year.

"A little harder Bags, maybe you need to hit the gym. Get to work on those pythons." There was something about these boys. They carried such confidence yet had no established direction or dreams in life. Then again, who was I to talk. Here was "Bags," openly carrying his doubt, depression and, cynicism, topped with half of a lifetime of schooling, a master's degree, whipped cream and a cherry.

My biggest dream in life was to catch a record fish from one of the local DNR fisheries. Not much different than these three boys whose daily goal was to meet a new girl and get a new phone number. In fact, that was their standing bet, and the loser bought beer after work every Friday. Maybe they did have more goals and desires to win than I did. So, I'll say it again, who was I to criticize?

As I walked in the back door, I passed Danny, who was catching up on the dishes he didn't complete after the dinner rush on Saturday. Johnny had called Danny that morning and in a not-so-pleasant early morning tone, encouraged him to join the team on the eight o'clock shift. Although it was a Monday, it was going to be busy, as it was the winter festival week for the local Catholic Church. Johnny always ensured that pizzas were continually stocked to help the church with their pizza sale. It was going to be a busy week and, as Johnny used to say, a spiritually profitable week. I had never really understood what he meant by that, but I would grow to understand later. Johnny's family had been helping the church for nearly the entire time they had been in business. Father DeFalco helped Johnny through a rough time when he lost his Dad, Nunzio, and he has never forgotten it. I am not sure how old Father DeFalco is, but every year I think that he is not going to make it another one. He shuffles along at his own speed, and I am not sure if he is always smiling or if his face is just stuck like that. Nonetheless his expression somehow lightens my heart.

When I first met Father DeFalco he said I was one of the

few in the world that knew how to make this red sauce and before he died, he would get me to tell him the recipe. I told the good Father that I know Johnny loves him, but if I ever gave him the recipe, I'd get my shoes replaced with cement blocks or my car tuned up. Tuned up is what it was called when the Italian mob decided to wire your car to explode when you started it. Father DeFalco got the hint about how important the recipe was to the Prezioso family, but it never stopped him from asking.

That morning Father DeFalco shuffled into the restaurant and wandered back into the kitchen to say hello. He slowly made his way towards me.

"Hey Bags, good to see you this morning my friend, I need a favor from you, and you will be honored in God's eyes if you could help this old priest out," he said.

"Sure, Father DeFalco, what can I help you with?" I replied. He slid a notebook across the stainless-steel prep table.

"Write that damn recipe down or I'm gonna tune up your car," he said, as only Father DeFalco could. He hunched over slightly and began a joyous laughter. We both busted out in laughter. To hear the old priest use a cuss word, as tame as it may have been, was quite a treat. I let him know I respected his persistence and desire, but I had an obligation to the Prezioso family to protect the recipe. I told him that I hoped that God would look favorably upon that. With a little chuckle, the Father replied, "I am sure he does Joey; I am sure he does." This made me smile because somehow, I was comforted by the fact that Father DeFalco confirmed my action was favorable in God's eyes. It made me feel really good even though I wasn't even sure I believed in God or the existence of a higher power. Nonetheless, the good Father made me smile and that is something I don't take lightly.

Speaking of people who could make me smile, Johnny entered the kitchen from the back door as Father DeFalco and I continued to laugh. As he walked by the dishwasher near the back door. "Happy you could make it to work today, Danny. It is always a pleasure to see young men like you anxious to work in the morning," he said. Danny was a special kid who suffered from some mental disorders and had fits every now and then, even though he was medicated. In response to Johnny's greeting, Danny let out a loud outburst that sounded like, "Son of a bitch." Johnny never missed a step. "Now Danny, you know I love you and I am helping you to be a better man, and, as well, you are helping me. Keep up the great work buddy," he said.

Johnny had an uncanny way of coaching and mentoring young men. The young guys in the restaurant loved Johnny even though sometimes they didn't appreciate his challenges. They could see the fruit it was bearing in their lives and really appreciated what he was doing for them. He was a true father figure to those boys. Johnny and I had known each other for over fifteen years and he was a major reason I made it through some rough times. Many years ago, I was just a customer, but to Johnny, everyone was a friend. He took me under his wing and even as a guy that has a master's degree working in a pizza shop, I am thankful for all he has done for me.

Certain moments happen in your life that change everything, often times you don't even recognize them. Often times you may not notice how truly special something was, and you may not recognize it for years. What was about to happen between Johnny, Father DeFalco and I was one of those moments.

CHAPTER TWO

THE RECORD BREAKER

Johnny walked up to us and asked if we were up to no good. I assumed he asked because Father DeFalco and I were still grinning from our earlier antics. Both the Father and I looked at each other. "Nope," Father Defalco answered simply. Johnny looked at both of us suspiciously but moved on with his conversation. Johnny acknowledged the weather, asked how things were going at the church, and how Sister Margo was doing. Sister Margo was another one of the clergy members that had quite an impact on Johnny when Nunzio passed away. She doesn't come around the restaurant much because her stomach can't handle the acid in the tomatoes, but she can't say no. She told Johnny every time she saw him how she loved his sauce, but she paid for eating it every time.

Johnny continued with small talk and I stayed out of the conversation. Then Johnny asked Father DeFalco if he had broken any records lately. "Nope, but the record I landed in 1989 still stands," he said.

My curiosity got the better of me. "What record are you referring to Father DeFalco?" I asked.

"Oh Bags, it is nothing big unless you like to fish." *Did the old priest just say what I think he said?*

"Are you kidding me?" I said. "Fishing is my second real passion in life and owning a lake record is probably one of my biggest goals right now. Actually, it has been a goal of mine for the last fifteen years." I really said my second passion because Johnny was standing right there, and I didn't want him thinking I wasn't dedicated to the restaurant. The truth was that fishing was probably my number one passion in life.

The Father chuckled. "Well, just another thing we have in common, Bags. You dream to hold a lake record, and I have held six local lake records for both walleye and crappie. Only one remains though, that is the eleven-pound fourteen-ounce walleye record for Mosquito Lake which I caught in 1989."

I turned my attention to Johnny. "And you knew this, Johnny?" I asked.

Here was a man I had known for years. I had enjoyed for years. All this time I never knew he was one of the best fishermen in Northeast, Ohio. Heck, for all I knew at that time, he may have been one of the best in the whole state. For goodness sake, owning six lake records is no easy feat. "Yes, I knew this," Johnny said. "My dad and Father DeFalco fished together often. Growing up as a kid, I remember a lot of stories from the two of them, and Mom complaining because Dad wouldn't come home for three days straight sometimes. She always said she couldn't complain because he was spending time with one of the best men she had ever known. Dad told Mom all the time that Father DeFalco was teaching him to catch fish and cast lines."

The good Father chuckled. "Johnny, you sure do have a good memory. I always said when you are on the water you should expect to catch, and when introducing people to the gospel, you simply cast lines. Either way, you have no control over the situation, you just do what you think is right," he said.

"I am sure glad you and Dad were so close," said Johnny. "You helped make him a great man."

"I didn't make him anything, but I introduced him to the one that did." The old priest chuckled and grinned. "And as a bonus we caught some really big fish."

At this point, all I could think about was whether he could or would share his spots and secrets. I was so taken aback by the whole conversation that I didn't know what to say next. I am sure I looked like I was in shock. I reached up and put my hand on my heart to make sure it wasn't going to pound out of my chest. Johnny looked at me and asked if I was okay. "Yes, Johnny, I'm fine. Just trying to gather my thoughts," I said.

Johnny looked at me strangely. "Well don't spend too much time gathering your thoughts, you have red sauce to make and Father DeFalco is counting on you. Isn't that right Father?" he said. Father DeFalco nodded, and Johnny headed to the front of the restaurant where he took his station behind the front counter. Father DeFalco stayed right where he was. I believe he sensed that I wanted to continue the conversation.

The Father wasted no time. "Bags, I am not sure why you struggled trying to hide your passion for fishing, or why you found it necessary to play down your excitement. Let it out my friend. One thing I've learned from the confession booth over the years is how to read emotion in a person's voice. You, my friend, love the art of fishing, and for this you should be proud."

So, it's probably pretty obvious how I got my nickname now. There is an old saying that some people wear their emotions on their shirt sleeve. I have a habit of wearing mine plastered on the chest, the sleeves, and the back of my shirts. But I realized that showing that emotion may have benefitted old Bags this time since I was about to pry open a can of secrets and techniques that had helped the good Father master his art and firmly plant himself in the record books. I wasn't about to let this one get away.

I began by asking, "Father, would you be willing to share some of your secrets or give me some tips?" I have never been known to dance around the topic, I get straight to the point. Father DeFalco stared into my eyes and pulled himself uncomfortably close.

"The man who won't show me how to make his pasta sauce now wants something from this old priest. What an interesting turn of events," He said in a creepy Jack Nicholson or Anthony Hopkins-like tone that made my skin tingle. Then after a really awkward moment of silence he whispered, "Of course I will Bags, it would be my pleasure." He chuckled, turned around, and shuffled towards the double kitchen doors. My mind was spinning. I was about to make great strides towards fulfilling my obsession.

"So, when will you tell me Father DeFalco?" I yelled as if he was one hundred feet away. It was the strangest thing; he didn't even respond to me. I thought maybe he didn't have his hearing aids turned up or he had second thoughts about telling me. I watched him walk through those kitchen doors and shuffled to the front to say goodbye to Johnny. Just then, I looked down and realized my apron was still spotless. It was 9:15 and I hadn't even started the sauce, but I had just had what seemed like the most exciting encounter of my life and I wasn't sure where to go next.

Over the next ten hours at work my mind became overwhelmed with thoughts. I wondered where Father DeFalco's "honey holes" might be. I was envisioning a beautiful spring morning, fog rising from the lake. I thought about what his favorite baits may be. Was he a live bait fisherman? Did he like to throw crankbaits? Was he fond of trolling? Were jigs or drift fishing his favorite techniques? I had so many questions and I couldn't wait to see the good Father again to continue our conversation. Each time I heard the bell on the front door of the restaurant, I walked over to look through the windows on the double doors of the kitchen. The day seemed to drag on forever as we made pizza after pizza for the church. I was hoping at some point the Father would come to pick up some pizzas, but I knew that was a far cry. There were plenty of young men helping out with the festival and I knew they were the ones who would show up to pick up the pizzas. That day I made twenty-seven gallons of red sauce and we produced 125 pizzas for the church while serving a steady lunch crowd, plus a somewhat light early dinner crowd. It was usual for our dinner crowds to be light during the church's winter festival because it was a strong draw on our normal clientele. Nonetheless, my mind was not fully committed to making red sauce because it was too consumed with dreams of Saturday morning adventures on the lake. I couldn't wait to finish up and call Scott to tell him the exciting news.

Around 7:00 p.m. I decided to call it a day. Johnny was gone so I slipped out the back door. Scott and his new wife Kim lived about seven miles from the restaurant and I decided rather than trying to call, I would swing by his house with this amazing news and tell him in person. It was still incredibly cold outside, and my Cutlass was taking a while to warm up and defrost the windows. I was feeling amazing, though. I had envisioned that spring morning so much that my body didn't even recognize the cold.

"What an amazing day," I heard myself say out loud, as I pulled away from the restaurant. As I pulled up to Scott's house, I didn't see any lights on, and hoped it wasn't a wasted trip. He had a long blacktop driveway with rows of evergreen bushes on both sides. As I got closer to the house, I could clearly tell no one was home. There wasn't a single light on in the house and no cars in the driveway. My car lights shined in the garage windows and I could see that there were no cars inside, so I didn't even get out. I put the car in reverse and again heard myself say, "I'll call him when I get home."

When I got to my duplex, I saw my neighbor putting salt down on the driveway on her side. She waved and I nodded in return, heading straight for the front door to get inside and call Scott. At the time, I didn't have a cell phone because I didn't believe in them, but I knew Scott did and I should be able to reach him wherever he was. I went inside, threw my keys on the kitchen table, reached for the phone on the wall and began dialing. The phone rang three times and I heard Scott answer the way he always does when I call.

"Fish On."

"You have no idea what happened to me today, you are going to be thrilled," I immediately said. I am sure Scott sensed the happiness in my voice, especially that was quite unusual after a long, cold winter. I went on to spill my story to Scott about the Father, the fishing records, the willingness to share his secrets, and the details of our conversation. The more I talked the more silence I heard on the other end, but it didn't seem to matter. I just kept talking and talking until I stopped myself and asked Scott if he was still there.

"Wow! Yes, Bags I am still here. Have you been drinking cappuccinos at work again?" He asked. I chuckled and finally asked Scott what he has been up to.

Scott told me that he and Kim were expecting their first child. I was blown away and excited for him until I realized how much that might change how often we would get to fish together. So, I asked all the right questions. When is she due? Do you guys know what you are having? I had to intentionally sound excited to cover up what I was really thinking. Scott said they were having a boy, and Kim was due in August.

"Joey, I know you far too well and know what you are really thinking, and I have to tell you something more," Scott said. I could tell by the tone of his voice what was coming next was not going to be good. He told me that he was sorry he didn't have time to call me, but over the winter his company had relocated him to Montgomery, Alabama. The company purchased his house and they moved right away. I remember the moment of silence more clearly than anything that was said. It seemed like a good five minutes, but I am sure it was really something like fifteen seconds. This would explain why the house looked so empty...because it was.

So, here I am with an opportunity to catch the biggest fish of my life, and my best friend is no longer around to share the moment. It seems I never find harmony with all things. I supposed I would be spending quite a bit of time alone on the water this year. First thing's first, I need to know Father DeFalco's spots.

CHAPTER THREE

FOUNDATION

The next few weeks seemed to go on forever. The restaurant was consistently busy, and I had pretty much come to grips with the fact that Scott was not going to be around in the spring. I found myself staying active with the tasks of running Prezioso's, yet my mind, and definitely my heart, was not fully committed. Actually, there was an incident where young Nick was pouring sauce into the plastic freezing tub, and he found that I had left a wooden spoon in the sauce.

"Hey Bags, you're losin' it, pal," he teased. "It's only a matter of time before Johnny has to teach me the recipe because you can't remember to put your pants on in the morning." I chuckled and snapped back at him with my own usual wit, but inside I wondered if he was right. Then I realized that it was because I was thinking about the coming spring.

Johnny had been away. He took a few days off like he did after every church festival. I used to think it was because he worked so hard preparing for the festival and he needed time to regain his strength, but these days the staff does most of the work. I figured that because the festivals were so important to Nunzio, he must spend the entire time reflecting on his dad and the church, and it simply wore him out. Whatever the reason, I certainly didn't mind stepping in and making sure the restaurant ran as expected so people came in hungry and left with smiles. I often wanted to ask Johnny where he went during these times because he always came back super refreshed and overly generous. One year he took a week and a half off after the summer festival and he came back and gave the entire staff bonuses for taking care of the place while he was gone. Nick and Tino jokingly spread rumors that Johnny went to Vegas and hit it big. Johnny caught wind of the rumors and the next week, Nick and Tino's paychecks suddenly showed just one dollar with a note that said, "Last week I hit it big, this week I lost it all. I hope you don't mind! Love Johnny." Of course, after some great laughter he had their real paychecks ready to go. I was eager to see how Johnny felt when he returned this time because the church had thrown its best festival to date, raising nearly $75,000, and we had been a big part of that.

I hadn't seen Father DeFalco in what seemed like months but in reality, it had been three weeks since he said he would share his secrets. It was starting to warm up a little and most of the snow has melted. One day that week it almost made it to forty degrees, and it may be not be a coincidence that it was the day I had left the spoon in the sauce. My mind had gone through the ups and downs of making each member of the restaurant staff my fishing partner. Young Nick, any of that crew in fact, would drive me crazy, calling me out on every bad cast. Danny would be yelling obscenities and scaring away the fish. Johnny would never be consistent and would cancel often. Our food server Julie would probably be the best choice, but I can't see her willingly getting dirty or baiting her own hooks. I concluded that I would definitely be fishing alone, but I accepted it.

It was March 24. I think it was a Tuesday. That previous weekend I had found myself at the local tackle shop where I spent about thirty-five dollars. I probably shouldn't have spent it, but I felt it would improve my chances of catching the record. I did this without guidance from Father DeFalco because I hadn't seen him. I was standing in the front of the restaurant counting the register before the dinner rush hit. This was the normal routine. I would count the money after the lunch rush, document everything in a logbook, keep what was needed in the drawer for change for our dinner crowd, put the rest in a large blue vinyl bank envelope, and lock it in the restaurant office. We had a great lunch that day. It had warmed up to forty-five degrees and was unusually sunny. People were out and about, and the restaurant seemed to benefit.

As I was counting the twenty dollar bills, I heard the old bell ring as the door opened, but I continued to count. I had a bad habit of counting out loud and that is exactly what I was doing when around the corner shuffled Father DeFalco.

"Put that money down son or I'll call the police," he yelled. Normally I would have been frustrated with anyone who made me lose my count but, in that case, I couldn't have cared less.

"Well hello there, great vanishing man of God. So happy to see you are still on this side of the dirt," I said to him.

Father DeFalco chuckled. "I can't say that I am thrilled about it, but I talked to God last night and He said it wasn't my time. He said I have a promise I must fulfill first."

"What was that promise?" I asked him.

The old man looked at me and smiled. "Well if you don't want to catch that record fish, I will talk to him again tonight."

I responded quickly. "I was hoping you were gonna say that.

You aren't going anywhere. Okay, stop bothering me because I have to count this money for the dinner rush or Johnny will have my neck. Help yourself to the world's greatest cup of coffee, you know where it is."

I finished counting each tender twice and went back to lock it in the office. I came back out into the restaurant and Father DeFalco was scribbling on a napkin. I sat down with him.

"So where are you, Bags?" he asked. I had no idea what he meant by that.

"I'm right here sir. I'm not sure I understand," I responded simply.

He chuckled. "Of course, you are right here my dear friend, but where is your mind and what have you prepared? The ice is almost completely off the water. You asked me to show you my secrets and I agreed. I thought you would have a foundation laid out for us by now."

Now I have been fishing for many years and I would consider myself a good angler, but I could not figure out what the good Father was saying. All I could think of was to tell him about Scott moving away, and how I don't have a truck to haul my boat. I poured the whole story out to him in what felt the world's longest run-on sentence.

"Boy oh boy," he replied. "I guess we have some work to do. No wonder God turned me away from the door." I awkwardly chuckled because I had no idea if he was referring to me personally needing a lot of help, or what.

"Father, I'm sorry, but I'm not keeping up with you. What are you trying to say?" I asked. Although I had never heard Father DeFalco preach a sermon, I could tell by the look in his eye that he was either about to give me a private demonstration or he was going to just shake his head and leave.

Father DeFalco continued to scribble on the napkin and I was growing anxious. I was ready to hear the sermon because I didn't want to wait another three weeks before seeing the good Father again. Finally, he began, "Bags, I need you to listen up, I am about to give you the best fishing lesson you have ever heard. And by the look in your eyes during our conversation, I believe you have been missing this for all these years. If you focus on this, you will not only catch more fish, but you will gain a new perspective of the world around you. Are you ready for the first and number one rule for fishing and life?"

I probably looked like a Labrador retriever drooling while others ate dinner. Not only was I ready, a puddle of drool was forming below me as I thought about the first real lesson. Then he spoke one word.

"Foundation."

There was an odd moment of silence. "What?" I finally replied. Then came the sermon, or what I thought one of his sermons may be like. He put both hands on the table, pushed himself to his feet and stated it again.

"Foundation." He paced two steps or, should I say shuffles, in each direction. Passion exuded from him and I was all ears.

"Bags, I have to tell you that I am rather disappointed," Father DeFalco began, "but it is not your fault. You have probably never been taught what it takes to reach things that seem unreachable. I realized a few things in our brief conversation this morning. I realized I will not be able to just tell you about my most successful spots, or the bait I used to catch the record-breaking fish. You, my friend, are longing for those secrets because although you have put forth great effort, you are probably not much closer at achieving that goal today than the first time you launched a boat in those waters. My first question to you today was a set-up. I now clearly see where we must begin."

I watched Father DeFalco pace back and forth six times without saying a word. He was rubbing his chin and hands together as though he were masterminding a fiendish plot. "I purposely gave you three weeks so I could see where you were with laying the foundation for the upcoming season when I returned."

"Write these things down," he said, handing me a napkin. I wrote down what he said:

Foundation

Target

Strategy

Suddenly, it felt as if I went from a sermon about fishing to being back at Cleveland State about to start another master's thesis. Either way, I was very intrigued, waiting to see what was next.

"Bags, you are a really smart guy. I am going to give you two days and I am going to come back and see where you are.

I want you to describe to me in detail what you believe the foundation is for your upcoming fishing season. The foundation is everything right now, and we have to move quickly because the ice is melting," Father DeFalco said.

I shook my head. "This is definitely the strangest fishing lesson I have ever had but I will give it my best."

The good Father shuffled towards the front door, chuckling. "I know you will, Bags, that is exactly why Johnny and I love you. Oh yeah and the big guy upstairs loves you too." He was about to open the door, but turned around, adding, "oh yeah, one hint. Bags, flip your napkin upside down. see how the foundation supports the other two? Yes, it is first and most important, but when action is set in place, your foundation must support the target you are trying to hit and the strategy you use to hit it. Make sure you think that one through. You can't build a house on sand. Also, when I get back, tell me which of these three steps we do on the water. We start fishing now."

He turned and opened the door wider this time and stopped again. "Oh yeah, I am sorry to hear that your friend moved away but when I come back, I don't want to hear about any challenges in which you are not in control. You are in complete control of building your foundation. Build it good, make it stable and ensure it supports the rest of the list. See you in a couple of days."

"See you, Father DeFalco!" I shouted. The first dinner party arrived, taking advantage of the Father holding the door open for them, and I grabbed some menus to seat them.

I worked the front of the restaurant the rest of the night which I really enjoyed. Greeting our customers, laughing, smiling, and of course thinking often about my conversation with Father DeFalco. I wouldn't let him down. I couldn't wait until I had time to really think about the words he had me write on the napkin. It was in my pocket and I pulled it out a few times during the evening to read it. The next day was my day off, and I had planned to spend as much time as possible working on my thoughts, and as Father DeFalco explained, building the foundation for an amazing fishing adventure.

I found it amazing that three simple words written on a napkin had my mind spinning in circles as much as it did. They were just three words, but I had to keep pulling the napkin out of my pocket and read them again and again like I couldn't remember what the good Father had said. Every time I read, it seemed to trigger different thoughts. At one point in the evening one of our regular clients, Joe, walked up to the front counter to talk with me about one of the nightly specials, and he found me standing with my back turned to the register, in deep thought, staring out the front window of the restaurant. He politely cleared his throat to get my attention. I snapped out of it, turned around, and apologized.

"No problem Bags," he said. "It seems there is a great deal on your mind my friend. Anything you want to talk about? Everything okay?"

"Oh yeah, Joe, everything is fine. I was just reflecting on a conversation I had with Father DeFalco earlier. He's a good man," I replied.

Joe told me that he felt the kitchen staff was putting too much fresh basil in the Frutti di Mare special we had on the menu tonight. He said that Johnny used to make the dish for him all the time and it was never quite so sweet and green. I did what Johnny would always do for someone who had a complaint; I took it off his bill. I also walked back to the kitchen and had a talk with the guys about how they were making the dish. They all understood and apologized while never lifting their eyes from the line. We still had many tables to serve in the dining room and they were in a strong sauté rhythm.

On the way back out of the kitchen, I pulled out the napkin and read those three words once again. Foundation, target, and strategy... Foundation, target, and strategy. What did the old man mean? How does it apply?

The rest of the night we kept up a great pace, and I was certain Johnny was going to be happy because we had some of our biggest spenders in the restaurant that night. Our servers were really happy, especially Julie, who at one point had three six-top tables full of premier diners who tipped her really well. It wasn't surprising because Julie was one of those efficient servers who never gets rattled and makes everyone's dining experience better. If you remember earlier, I said she would be my best choice for a fishing partner, but I just couldn't see her agreeing to it.

At 12:40 or so, the restaurant was cleared out and Danny was done washing dishes and mopping floors, and we were ready to go. The young Italian boys were heading to "the strip" to try and pick up some girls. I let the testosterone-overloaded teenagers out the back door before locking up and going out the front. Thankfully, tomorrow was my day off. As the good Father said earlier, "We start fishing now."

CHAPTER FOUR

A DAY OFF

The next morning, I woke up excited about deciphering the words written on that napkin. Never before have I put so much thought into three simple words. I woke up around 3:30 a.m. the night before, wondering why I was so consumed with thought. Was it because the challenge came from one of the best men I have ever known? Was it because I thought it would get me the best chance at a lake record? Was it just because I was starting to get the spring itch to get on the water? I came to no conclusion, so I went back to sleep, but my mind never let it go. I just kept repeating those words in my mind over and over again. As I started to prepare the coffee pot that morning, I wondered how many times I had said the word "foundation" in my mind. I quickly gathered an old notepad and pen and was ready to get started putting my thoughts on paper to share with the good Father. I wandered to the chair at the end of the kitchen table. I remembered my Grandfather calling the chair at the end of his kitchen table his thinking chair. It was the best seat to sit in that morning. My Grandpa would sit in his thinking chair for hours, drinking Koehler Beer and eating peanuts. He had a little dog named Dude, and he and Dude would share peanuts as Grandpa would sit and think. I never knew what he was thinking about but any time I would ask he would say, "nothing...just thinking." Now was my turn to just think, and I was hoping I would have some good thoughts.

The foundation...what was Father DeFalco referring to when he said foundation? I struggled with this for nearly an hour before I finally felt like I established a direction. The hardest part of this exercise was the fact that I was constantly thinking about what Father DeFalco was thinking. I knew the good Father fairly well, but not enough to understand his thought patterns. I reflected upon what he said when he was leaving. He stopped and turned around to tell me to flip the napkin upside down and recognize that the foundation supported both the target and strategy. I thought about what I was going to need to support my goal of catching a record breaker, and the strategy I was hoping Father DeFalco was going to help me build. Because God knows I had been trying for years and although I had caught some good ones, I had nothing close to a record.

I built a list of everything I was going to need. This is what I assumed he meant by foundation. First off, I was going to need a boat or a way to haul my flat bottom. Since Scott was no longer around, I had lost my transportation. I supposed I could put racks on my Cutlass, but I was not sure how to do that. Nonetheless, this is where I was starting my list.

Foundation:
- Boat (could take flat bottom on roof racks) Need Roof Racks
- Light Action, Medium Action and Heavy Action Spinning Combos
- Wide Range of Tackle (Spinners, Live Bait Rigs, Crankbaits)
- Rod Holders
- Fish Finder
- Trolling Motor

I finished writing my list and I felt pretty good. I probably read it thirty times and couldn't think of anything I was missing. If I had all of these things, many which I did already, I would be ready to go. I sure hope this is what the good Father was talking about when he said foundation. If I didn't have any of these things, I couldn't even get on the water, so I would call this the foundation. One minute I felt confident and the next minute I was unsure. At one point, I chuckled to myself because I couldn't believe I was so worried about being wrong. I am not sure I was ever this worried at any point in my entire college career. I guess I just didn't want to let Father DeFalco down. After all, he was going to help me live out my dream.

Then I started the next list. I quickly realized that it wasn't going to be a list at all. This was going to be more like a mission statement. And that would come easily, because I had been thinking about this my whole entire life. I wrote:

Target: My goal and mission is to catch a record-breaking.

Ding dong...Ding dong. I couldn't believe it. The doorbell was ringing. I was right in the middle of penciling my lifelong goal and mission. Who in the world is it and can't they come back? The doorbell kept ringing, so I put my pencil down and went to answer it. I opened the door to see my next-door neighbor. She was really upset and had a little one in her arms, and another holding her hand. They looked very cold.

"I know we don't really know each other, but I lost the key to my apartment and I called a locksmith. We've been standing outside for an hour waiting on him and we are freezing. Can we wait inside?" she asked. As much as I wanted to say that I was busy, their rosy red cheeks and runny noses made me feel like I couldn't say no to the three of them.

"Sure, you can wait in here. I don't have much, but I do have some coffee, would you like me to make a pot?" I offered.

"Sure, that would be nice. My name is Megan, and these are my sons Jimmy and Joey," she said awkwardly as she bent over to remove clothing from her boys, who were not cooperating. Having very little experience, in fact, no experience with kids, I kept my distance and began making coffee. After all, in a strange way, she seemed to have it all under control.

"Well let me go ahead and get some coffee started," I said, walking to the kitchen. "Megan, you said one of your boys name is Joey. That's my name too, but my friends call me Bags. It's a long story," I continued as I started the coffee in the pot. I turned around to see the three had joined me in the kitchen.

Honestly, I never paid much attention to them before and Megan was quite attractive. Her little boys were good looking little guys even with rosy cheeks, runny noses and hair matted from their stocking caps. She responded to my introduction with a confident, strong handshake. "It's nice to finally meet you Joey, we appreciate your kindness."

"No problem, I was just sitting around, and wasn't doing anything real important," I said, and nearly bit my tongue off. The truth was it was probably the worst timing ever, and all I wanted to do was complete the good Father's tasks.

The boys appeared considerably uncomfortable and stood

very close to Megan. Her smallest one, Jimmy, seemed to have himself permanently attached to her hip. He would not stray far from her, and he kept looking me in the eye as if he was evaluating me, determining if he approved or not. Joey looked a little more comfortable, but still would not leave his mom's side. He seemed to be evaluating my belongings more than me. His eyes scanned the room. I could sense that his thought process was rapid like mine, but probably much less judgmental. The sound and smell of coffee began to fill the kitchen. A friend of mine, a barista in Georgia, recently discovered this amazing roasted blend from Cuba, and it was starting to cover up the smell of wet cold clothes and little boys. Everyone was starting to warm up. As the coffee aroma filled the room and I gathered the cups and accessories, I noticed Megan's body language showed signs of comfort.

Her boys were still hesitant, so I asked them if they would like some chocolate milk or Kool-Aid. I very rarely buy chocolate milk, but luckily, I had bought half a gallon the day before because it was on sale and had appealed to my inner child. I always kept Kool-Aid in the refrigerator. It was something I had continued from my home growing up. Orange was the flavor of the day and neither boy wanted that, so I poured them some chocolate milk as I waited for the coffee to finish brewing. Megan was thankful as I handed Joey his glass of milk and I handed her Jimmy's because he was still visibly uncomfortable interacting with me. She took the glass and coaxed both of the boys towards the table. The boys sat down and she told Jimmy to sit up straight in the chair while I asked how she took her coffee.

"There is no need to prepare my coffee, I can make my own," she said as she settled the boys in at the table and quickly turned to step back into the kitchen with confidence and assertiveness, characteristics I was not used to in myself, let alone in an attractive young mom. I have a very small kitchen in my duplex, but Megan had no issues rubbing elbows and asserting herself in my space as she went about preparing her coffee. She was maybe five foot two, but she held herself as confidently as a six-footer. She was tiny, maybe one hundred pounds, but she had a presence about her that made her appear much larger. Although she was very feminine, she carried herself as if she was in complete control, and she had a little growl in her voice that made you think she would bite if you weren't careful. My mind had already wandered to thoughts about Joey and Jimmy's dad, but I also knew better than to begin with those questions or we'd only get half a cup swallowed before she'd run.

Megan finished making her coffee and sat down across from me at the table.

"Bags huh? Sounds like an interesting story. No need to go there this morning, but I will get there before long. That is, of course, if I get invited back," she said. I was still trying to make that assessment myself. After all, she was interrupting the most exciting thing that has happened to me in quite a few years. Nonetheless, I remained cordial and neighborly as we continued to get to know each other.

The boys had made their way into the living room where they discovered the old Nintendo 64 game system I had hooked up. Before long, they were completely occupied by the 1990's 64-bit graphics and the dated sounds of arcade games of the past. Megan noticed what was going on. "Bags, are you okay with the boys playing your game? I am sorry they attacked it, or at least I am assuming they attacked it." I let her know that they did not attack it, however I did see their eyes light up when they saw the game controllers and asked if they wanted to play.

"Well that was awful nice of you, and surprisingly attentive." she said. I looked back at her, not sure if that was a complement or some kind of jab at me. "Yes, Bags I was surprised, because we have lived next to you for quite some time and you have never seemed to notice us before," she said. "Honestly, I was quite hesitant to ring your doorbell, but now I am glad I did. I can see already that you are a good soul. Maybe a little bit of a loner but a good soul."

I was taken aback by Megan's whirlwind of perceptive enlightenment. It intrigued me, and I understood that I was dealing with a thinker. But all I kept thinking about was the foundation that Father DeFalco requested I define.

We continued to talk. I enjoyed having a conversation with someone who had a strong vocabulary, was opinionated but accepting of different views, and was not afraid to let out a few deep belly laughs. Most of all, she was not afraid to challenge me when I would slide into my "woe is me" mentality.

At one point she said, "oh boy, Bags, I never noticed you

wearing that skirt before." I guess she meant that I was being emotional like a female. That was probably fair, and it made me chuckle. I really liked her spunk and fortitude. Her boys remained occupied with game after game on my Nintendo. I would see her glance over my shoulder often to check on them and every now and then I would turn my head to make my own evaluation. The first moment of silence took place about forty-five minutes into their visit. Oddly enough, we chose to look awkwardly in opposite directions as if afraid to make eye contact without words spewing from our lips. In the midst of this uncomfortable moment, Megan noticed my notepad.

"Foundation, target?" she questioned. Just then her phone begins to play *Subdivisions* by Rush. That was her ringtone? I was completely taken aback. Rush was not only my favorite band but a reason I made it through some pretty tough times. That particular song had lyrics I really connected with.

She answered the phone. "Just give me a second, I am right next door. I'll be right there," she said, then hung up. "Okay boys, get your coats and hats on, we're gonna get back into the house," she said. The boys reluctantly obeyed, moving quickly to get dressed and out the door. Megan rinsed out her own cup as well as the ones her boys used and turned to me. She grabbed both of my arms just above my elbows as if to hold me still, looked into my eyes, and said, "Bags, we appreciate your kindness, and hope that in the future you choose not to ignore us. Isn't that right, boys?" I was stunned that this tiny-framed woman could manage to hold me still.

"I won't," I responded.

"Good," she said. She opened the door, pushing her boys in front of her out into the cold. As she and her boys stepped off of my front porch, she turned to me. "Now get back to building your foundation and setting your targets. I can tell it's killing you," she said.

CHAPTER FIVE

ABSENCE OF THOUGHT

After Megan and her boys left my place that evening, I was honestly astonished at the ease of the interaction that had taken place. It had been quite some time since I'd felt that comfortable with someone outside of work. It was somewhat easy being social at work. I guess that was because I considered it part of my job, and I couldn't let Johnny down, so social I was. But it didn't typically transfer to my behavior outside of the restaurant. No one knew this better than my coworkers, who had all learned this over the years. They simply stopped asking me to hang out after work. I always chocked it up to the fact that I simply don't like people. My mom used to tell me as a little boy that I was "spirited." I never really knew what she meant by that, and I still don't, but I believe it was her nice, southern way of saying I was hard to deal with. Like when she would say, "bless his heart," she really meant "what a moron." She also used to say that I would grow out of it and at this point, I am not sure if it's possible. That was okay for now because I had to get back to work. I found my notepad and began to expand on my earlier thought.

Target: My goal and mission is to catch a record-breaking fish at a Northeast Ohio fishery.

It was that simple. That was my target, my goal. The good Father was going to love to hear this, and in the end, Megan and the boys really didn't make me lose much time. I was glad they came over. I had really enjoyed their company. In fact, I was kind of disappointed in myself for not getting her phone number or making arrangements to hang out again. Of course, she lived right next door, so I guessed it wouldn't be too long before we saw each other again.

The next morning, I woke up to the sound of *In-Fisherman* reruns on the TV. I had apparently fallen asleep watching fishing shows, although I couldn't remember it. I listened to the sound of Al and Ron Linder teaching how to rig a drift line with walking sinkers for summertime walleye in Minnesota. I always watched them when I was growing up, and I remember thinking that they must fish in the best lakes in the world, because the lakes around here don't have fish like that.

I jumped out of bed, anxious to get to work. I was sure Father DeFalco would stop by today, and I could walk him through the foundation and target I had written. I jumped out of bed with more vigor that I had in years and found myself whistling as I prepared to shower. I chuckled at myself a couple of times because I never whistle, unless it is the "death march." Now, peppy little tunes were coming from my lips. Today was going to be an amazing day. I finished showering, grabbed my apron and headed off to the restaurant. I believed Johnny was going to be back today, and I hoped the good Father found a reason to stop in too.

It wasn't really cold that morning, but it was wet. The weather actually warmed up overnight and most of the snow had begun to melt away. My car always seemed to be challenged by different climate conditions. It had a sunroof and any good amount of moisture seemed too find its way inside, so it fogged up the glass from the inside and the outside. Nothing that the defrosters on high couldn't handle. Unfortunately, my defroster fan had a broken blade so as it rotated on high speed it sounded like a popcorn machine. Nonetheless, I cleared the windows and went on my way.

That morning I arrived at the restaurant early. I noticed that the youthful Italian trio had left their mark out back. Paper cups were laying out by the yellow parking posts they had used as stools. The question was, what were they drinking in those paper cups? Oh, to be young again. I left the mess and let myself in the back door. It would make for some fun banter and coaching when the boys arrived. Things were in disarray, as if the team had their hands full the night before. There was nothing better than a good rush of customers to make you feel alive– and leave the kitchen distressed. I had seen worse times, but it did need some tidying up, so I got to work on the kitchen. My mind raced thinking about Father DeFalco's reaction to my foundation and target. I was wildly nervous, like I was about to take a test. I kept asking myself why I felt so nervous because I didn't believe the old priest was testing me. Not that I knew of, at least. About fifty minutes into my working day, I caught the sound of a car pulling up out back. I assumed it was one of the kitchen help or maybe even Johnny getting an early start. And then it happened.

Father DeFalco walked into the door with that magic little shuffle and a smile that only he could carry. It was kind of a cross between John Travolta in his *Saturday Night Fever* era and Walter Matthau from *Grumpy Old Men*. I am sure he saw my eyes light up. "GOOD MORNING," I exclaimed with pure enthusiasm. He looked at me as if he wondered if those were my paper cups out back. I recognized that my excitement was probably a little intense, and I tried to tone it down, but I was not sure I could. "Well Father DeFalco, I did what you asked, and I think I have my foundation and target defined," I exclaimed with childlike passion.

"Well good, Joey. I love to hear the passion in your voice, but the words you chose tell me we already have some work to do," Father DeFalco responded. The words I chose? What did he mean?

The Father grabbed a stool and pulled it up to the very end of the stainless-steel prep table. "Did you bring your notepad, young man?" he asked, popping both elbows onto the table. "Let's get started."

I quickly ran to the coat rack, pulled the notepad out from my jacket, and ran back. Father DeFalco then explained to me that the notepad was going to serve as my plan and my lesson guide. He asked me to count to page twenty and write at the top of that page the words THE BEST FISHERMAN in all capital letters, and then underline the word BEST. Of course, I did just as he asked.

"Now, everything I ask you to write in this section I want you to number," he said. "Before you talk about your foundation and target, I want you to write this: Number one. Confidence ALWAYS comes with an absence of thought," he said.

He told me to capitalize the word always and underline it. I wrote those words exactly, then looked up from writing, somewhat dumbfounded. The Father sat silently, staring into my eyes, waiting for me to talk. So, I did. I told him I was confused and asked if he could help me understand. Of course, he obliged.

"Joey, earlier I mentioned the words you chose. This is important because your words convey your true emotions. Your actions will follow, and confidence comes with the absence of thought. It probably doesn't seem like much, but it is very important to your success on the water and elsewhere. Let me explain more. When you were excited to let me know of your progress earlier, you stated, 'I think I have my foundation and target defined.' This statement told me there is a lack of confidence in the work you have done. Remove the words 'I think' from that statement and just listen to how much more confident it sounds. You should have just said, 'I have my foundation and target defined.' Most importantly, it signifies your belief. The words 'I think' basically say, 'I am unsure if it is right,' which leads to unnecessary changes in strategy, changes in tactics, and a lack of confidence, which leads to failure. The words 'I think' tell me you haven't thought enough. Confidence comes with the absence of thought. When you no longer have to think because you know."

Wow. I could never have imagined that someone could read so much into something because of my word choice. The more I thought about it, he was right. He saw the nerves, the anxiety, and how unsure I was. He saw it all and we hadn't even talked about the foundation and target yet. I told the good Father how amazed I was, and that I would need his help to gain the confidence I needed to win. I asked if I could share my foundation and target ideas with him.

"Absolutely Bags, I would love to hear about it, but my good friend Johnny is paying you, which means I am stealing from my friend. And as close as I am to meeting my Lord and Savior, I ain't blowing it now," said the good Father. He turned and walked back towards the doors as Tino, the first of the young Italian trio, came through to get started on his shift. I greeted him with enthusiastically. *Buongiorno*, Tino. Are you ready to have an amazing day?"

"I think so," he replied. Father DeFalco and I looked at each other with a grin and shook our heads. This young Italian stud had a lot to learn. The fact was, so did I.

I shouted to Father DeFalco as he shuffled out the back door. "Father, when can we talk foundation and target?" So much wisdom had been instilled that morning that I had almost forgotten.

"Tomorrow night after you get off at five. We will get coffee. It'll be my treat...I think," he replied. He winked and walked through the door.

"Father how did you know I get off at five?" I shouted to him.

He chuckled. "Magic, Joey, magic. I magically read the schedule posted in the kitchen. Know your surroundings Joey. By the way, that is number two. write it down. Know your surroundings. Good day, my friend. See you tomorrow."

I went back to my page titled the "The Best Fisherman" and wrote it down. I wrote down the number two, and the words "Know Your Surroundings." I supposed this was kind of like my mom saying, "Bless his heart." Seemed pretty obvious—

pay attention to your surroundings, you moron. Nonetheless, I started to see that I may get a little more out of Father DeFalco than just a few fishing lessons. I thought I was ready to get started. Or rather...I was ready to get started.

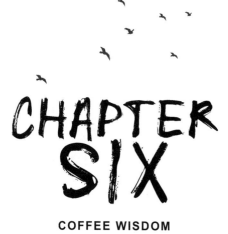

CHAPTER SIX

COFFEE WISDOM

The next day at work seemed to go on forever. It was red sauce day and I stayed busy, which usually makes the day go by fast, but not this time. At about noon I began watching the clock and I swear someone was playing tricks on me. What seemed like an hour turned out to be fifteen minutes. I even asked a few times to make sure the clock was right, and it was. I guess it was my anxiousness getting the best of me. At around two o'clock, Johnny came into the restaurant and he and I caught up in the office. Johnny and I had a special relationship and it always meant a lot to me that Johnny was willing to share his personal experiences with me. I didn't take it lightly, and I always kept our conversation in strict confidence. That afternoon, Johnny shared with me that he and his wife Dena had been arguing recently, and it was really bothering him. He recognized that his stubbornness was probably the biggest part of the problem, yet he couldn't seem to shake it. I think Johnny opened up to me because I let him think through things out loud without any suggestions at all. I never felt as if he was looking for answers from me, so I always just sat and listened until a span of silence would always end with Johnny saying something like, "Well Bags thanks for listening, I'm happy to have your friendship," and we would leave the office and go about our day.

Johnny's wife Dena was an amazing woman who grew up in Central Ohio on a small farm. When she visited the restaurant, she told stories of beheading and plucking chickens when she was a young girl. I could never imagine that because she is an incredibly beautiful woman. Not that girls who grow up on farms can't be beautiful, I guess I just couldn't imagine her killing her own food. I will tell you that it gave me a different perspective of Dena that I thought was pretty cool. With that said, I always imagined she could be a handful, or spirited, as my mom would say. It was not surprising that she wouldn't stand for Johnny's stubborn Italian way from time to time. That wasn't Johnny's fault either, he came from a long line of stubborn Italian men. However, those men were real pillars in our community.

When Johnny and I had time in the office that day, I told him that I was meeting Father DeFalco for coffee after work. "Wow, that's quite an honor. What's the occasion?" he asked. I told Johnny that Father DeFalco was going to share his fishing secrets with me. His eyes doubled in size. "That is something special, Bags, don't you take that for granted. He must think highly of you," Johnny said.

I told him that I most certainly wouldn't take it for granted, and Johnny went right back to discussing his uncertainty about his own behavior in his relationship with Dena. We sat and talked for nearly an hour, or rather, I sat and listened for nearly an hour. I did, however, have the opportunity to change the subject and ask Johnny if he ever fished with Father DeFalco.

"No, Bags, fishing was never my thing," Johnny told me. "My dad loved to fish, and he always tried to get me to like it, but I just didn't. That's why he and Father DeFalco fished together all the time. In fact, when my dad passed away, he left all of his equipment to Father Defalco in his will." I found this interesting, but I guess if he really didn't like to fish that made sense. I just couldn't imagine not liking fishing.

"Bags, I guess I should let you get back to work," Johnny finished. "I'm thankful for your friendship. I'm also happy to hear you are building a relationship with Father DeFalco. That will pay off for you in a big way." After my visit with Johnny, time slowed down again. The last two hours of my shift felt like four. My mind was revisiting my previous conversations with Father DeFalco and the list of needs that I had determined for my foundation. I also thought about the two lessons the Father had told me to write down on page twenty of my notepad. How did these things relate to me catching a record-breaking fish? All of this seemed very strange to me, but I couldn't deny the fact that the good Father held many records. As Johnny said, he was willing to spend time with me, and I couldn't take that for granted. It did make me feel kind of special that a guy of his stature would even acknowledge my presence, not to mention take the time to help me and share his secrets.

I looked up at the clock. It was 4:55, so I asked young Tino to finish up the vegetable prep I was working on. Although he grumbled and complained, he took the knife from my hand and continued the progress I had made. I thanked him, grabbed my coat off the coat rack, and double checked that my notepad was in the pocket. It was, so I threw my coat on and walked through the double doors to the front of the restaurant. Johnny was standing out front and I said goodbye to him as I walked towards the front door. The weather was nice, roughly sixty degrees and sunny. It was a tremendous spring day and a great day to talk fishing.

"Bags, did you hit your head? Your car is out back," Johnny said.

"I know where my car is, Johnny. Remember I told you I was meeting Father DeFalco for coffee?" I replied.

"Oh yeah. How could I forget. Tell the old priest I said hello, and enjoy your time, Bags," Johnny said as I left.

The restaurant was part of a plaza that was a center point for our community. In the plaza was a Hallmark store, a grocery store, a barber shop, an insurance agency, and the coffee shop. The coffee shop was called "The Spirited Bean," which used to make me chuckle, because of how my mom used to call me spirited. I had only been in the coffee shop a couple times because I was too cheap to pay what they were asking for a cup of coffee, but I would gladly pay it this time. In fact, I would probably pay double.

I walked into the coffee shop and was greeted by a young guy who was working behind the counter. "Welcome to the Bean!" he said. I thanked him as I looked around the room to see if the Father was already there. The young guy had a smile so big, I glanced down at myself to make sure my fly wasn't down, or something else out of place was making him smile. The shop was well lit, and apparently my excitement had caused me to arrive before the Father. I let the young man know that I was waiting on someone, but I ordered a large dark roast coffee, and asked him to bring it when my company arrived.

"No problem, take a seat anywhere, he said. "By the way, how are things at the restaurant?" he added. At first, I was confused and wondered to myself if I knew him. Then I realized I still had my work shirt on, and he must have noticed that when I unzipped my jacket.

"Things are good at the restaurant. Thanks," I responded, and I went to sit down at a small table for two.

As soon as I did, the bell on the front door rang and in shuffled Father DeFalco. He did not have his clerical clothing on, and, at first glance, I didn't recognize him. But it only took about five seconds to identify that unmistakable shuffle. The old man actually looked normal and I found this funny because, as long as I have known Father DeFalco, I have never considered him to be normal. After all, he was an honored and chosen man of God, and in my eyes, that is far from normal. He was looking quite rugged, He wore an old pair of jeans that looked like Wranglers, but with leather patches so worn that the brand was no longer legible. He had a bright orange T-shirt on, but you could only see the neck peeking out from under an army green sweater with a zipped-up collar. The sweater had a brown leather patch on the right shoulder that looked like it withstood a thousand concussive blows from a twelve gauge over the years. I was quite impressed with how "normal" Father DeFalco looked in these clothes. He was obviously comfortable and seemed much more approachable. He looked like many old men I see in those little sixteen-foot, well equipped aluminum boats at the lake. They always seemed to have the wisdom and knowledge I so desired, and I couldn't wait to start talking fishing.

"Good afternoon Father, you are looking very outdoorsy

today," the young man behind the counter said.

"Thanks Whit. It's a beautiful day, and I just couldn't bring myself to put on my monkey suit. I am meeting a friend here to talk fishing, and I felt like I needed to look the part."

"Fair enough Father," Whit replied, "and you most certainly look the part. Is your friend Joey? He sat down already." I could hear every word of their interaction and was wondering how this young man knew my name when I didn't remember introducing myself. Weird. I dismissed the thought and stood up to greet Father DeFalco with excitement.

I stopped and chuckled at myself when I realized I had walked nearly twenty steps from the table to greet the Father. I was obviously so excited to spend time with him that I couldn't wait for him to shuffle over to greet me.

"Hello Bags," the Father said as I approached. "It is a good day to plan some fishing. Do you agree?"

"Well Father, I was just thinking the same thing myself. The air smells so good, I love it when the seasons are changing," I said.

As we both sat down, I went straight for my coat pocket that had my notes. "Father I wrote down the foundation that I believe I need to be successful on the water, but I have to tell you that this was not easy. I wasn't really sure what you meant by foundation, so I hope I have it all thought out," I began.

"Well Bags, let's take a look," he replied.

As he spoke, I was already sliding the notebook over in front of him. I wondered if he would even be able to read it.

Although I was always a good student, but my handwriting was horrible. In grade school I would have straight A's except for writing, in which I would consistently get C's. Over the years, it never improved and in fact, the faster life got, the worst my writing became. Nonetheless, I slid the notepad in front of the Father to get his thoughts on my foundation. Much to my surprise, he had no issues reading my handwriting and started to read what I wrote out loud.

"Boat...yes, young friend, we definitely need that. However, if we did not have a boat it should not stop us. I have seen many records broken by fishing from shore. It proposes a challenge, but it's not impossible," he said.

"Fishing rods," he continued. "Yes, of course these are critical today, but I have seen some Hispanic gentlemen catching very large catfish down south in Georgia with a tin can and hand line, so we would still have a chance. Tackle. Of course, we need something for the fish to bite, but we shouldn't overthink it. I saw a young man catch a six-pound bass in our neighborhood pond on a hot dog. I learned my lesson as I attempted to coach this young man on how to use Texas rigged rubber bait, and he said confidently, without thinking, 'I've got this, watch.' And boy did he. She was a beautiful fish. Rod holders make it easier for sure. I am a fan of the fish finder and a trolling motor, and this is a pretty good list of things that can help us catch fish."

I was confused again. Was this the foundation he was looking for, or not? He seemed to be pondering it himself as Whit brought us our coffee and he took his first sip. There was a strange, awkward silence. I broke it by asking, "So what's next, Father? Should I work to get the things on this list that I don't have?"

"No worries Bags," the old man replied, finishing his sip of coffee. "I have everything you have listed here. We can do this together. You just keep burying your money in mason jars out back by your shed." He chuckled like the Father does from time to time. "Bags, do you believe great things can be done with very little?" he asked.

I was taken aback with the depth of what he was asking, and I pondered it for an extended amount of time. Now I was sipping my coffee. "Well Father, I guess in some instances that can be true, but not very often," I replied. The Father took another sip of coffee as he pondered my answer.

"I felt like you might answer that way. Bags, we are going to have some great times on the water. I have been looking for a new fishing partner since Johnny's dad went to join our Lord in Heaven, and I am so happy it is you," he said. Our conversation continued for quite some time, and the good Father continued to tell fishing story after fishing story. He talked about catching walleye in the Great Lakes, stripers in the south, groupers in the Panhandle, and on and on. I had no idea Father DeFalco was so well travelled, and his stories were amazing. He had a way of telling them that kept me hanging on every word. I could have sat there all night and listened to the old priest.

All of a sudden Father DeFalco stood up. "Well, Bags, it is time for this old man to go home," he said. I stood up to walk him to the door. The Father said hello to a young couple sitting on the couches and said his goodbyes to Whit. As we approached the front door, he stopped and turned to me.

"Bags, I appreciate you putting thought into what we need," he said. "It is a good list, but there is a very important thing you have forgotten for our foundation for success. After spending a little more time with you, I realize you would have never included it on your list, but that's why I'm here. I will teach you. I hope you will listen and learn, and we will catch some pretty darn good fish. Maybe even a record. If weather permits, we start fishing in two weeks, and we have work to do before then, so start thinking about your target and strategy. I noticed the target you had scratched on your pad and it isn't right. I want to know exactly what fish we are going after. If you don't clearly define your target, you never win. The next time we have coffee, we will discuss further. Get your notepad and scribble down some ideas. And write this down in your notepad Bags. Are you ready?"

I grabbed my notepad and pen. "The greatest piece of your foundation is oftentimes not visible or touchable, and you only know what you were missing once you've found it," he told me. I wrote that right below his other two one-liners.

1. Confidence Comes with Absence of Thought

2. Know Your Surroundings

3. The greatest piece of your foundation is oftentimes not visible or touchable, and you only know what you were missing once you've found it.

I still didn't see how any of this was going to help me catch a record, but I thanked Father DeFalco as he reached his arms out wide to give me a hug. He turned to shuffle back to his truck. I watched him, and then headed back to my car, feeling more excited and emotional than I had in years.

CHAPTER SEVEN

TARGET DISTRACTION

After leaving the Spirited Bean, I went back to the restaurant to get my car. I walked in the front door and the restaurant was hopping. Most of the food servers were clearly in the weeds and I knew if I stepped in to help, I would surely end up a target for frustration, so I swiftly moved through the front of the house and quietly scurried through the kitchen to get to my car. It was still a nice evening and it was good to see the back doors propped open with a bucket letting some air into the kitchen. This was a sure sign that spring was on the way. I was so ready for the weather to break and I was noticing all the signs those days. Father DeFalco said we were fishing in two weeks, weather permitting, and I couldn't wait to be taught some incredible techniques from the old man.

That drive home was an interesting one. I am typically not a passive driver, in fact, I am typically one of the more aggressive drivers on the road. When I have my mind set on getting somewhere, I am fervent about reaching my destination. My father taught me quite a few lessons and this was one that may have come from him.

I was born in a Naval hospital because my dad was in the military. Being prompt was bred into my very being growing up and getting somewhere early was like earning extra credit in my dad's eyes. As a child, I was doing all I could for extra credit because most often, I needed it. This evening, all of my thoughts seemed to blow out the window when I left the back parking lot behind the restaurant. In fact, at one point, I looked at the speedometer and realized I was going ten miles per hour below the speed limit.

I was revisiting story after story in my mind. Father DeFalco had shared a story about losing a crappie that he said was easily six pounds and could have been a world record. The way he described the fight, the action of the rod, the silver color of the fish, and of course, the translucent, paper mouth that gave way when he attempted to lift it into the boat, was amazing. He had a way of telling stories that kept me mesmerized.

As I turned onto my street, I could see Megan's car lights on in the driveway. Ever since she spent time at my house, when she locked herself out, we have been more cordial with each other, but neither of us had made any attempt to get together again. I saw young Jimmy standing on their front porch the other morning and I said hello, but he just looked at me and nodded his head. I didn't think much of it because I wasn't a super talkative kid at his age either.

I pulled in the driveway and Megan waved as if I was a long-lost relative coming to visit. I waved back, but also had cemented plans in my mind to get inside and get started on the next assignments from the Father. Target and strategy. I pulled forward in the driveway and before I came to a stop, Megan was at my door. I opened the door and she pleaded, "Bags, I'm so glad you are here. Do you know anything about cars? Because my car will not start. and I'm supposed to have my boys at school in twenty minutes to meet their art teacher."

"Well Miss Megan, let me take a look." I said. I noticed the lights on the car from the end of the street, so there must be plenty of power in the battery. As I sat in the car, I attempted to turn the key. The key turned but the car made no attempt to start. I reached down and pushed the button on the automatic floor shifter, and it popped forward into park. I turned the key again and became the hero. Megan was so excited, but a little embarrassed at the same time. Nonetheless, she gave me the biggest hug and a cute little kiss on the cheek that made me blush. She quickly got her boys in the car and headed on her way. "I will stop over later Bags. Thanks again!" she yelled out the window as she pulled out of the driveway.

I waved and unlocked my front door to find my place just like I left it. That is pretty much the way it is every time I come home. No surprises for Bags. If I don't do the dishes, they don't magically get done while I am out and about. I set down my backpack on the base of the coat rack near my front door and headed into the kitchen. Since I was going to start working on my next assignment, I decided to make a pot of coffee. Yes, I did have several cups at the Bean, but I was committed to continuing my caffeine intake as I defined the next steps laid out by the good Father.

I got the coffee started, but realized I left my notepad in my coat pocket and walked back to the coat rack in the front to find it. As I retrieved the notepad from my jacket pocket, I saw lights from a car turning into my driveway. Who could that be? I looked out the small window in my front door. It was Megan coming back, pulling into my side of the driveway. She had really good timing. Every time I planned to work on my assignments, she showed up. Although I was a little frustrated, I was also happy she came back. I heard her knock on the front door. I chuckled because there was a lighted doorbell that she just ignored, and this little pint-sized girl knocked hard enough to rattle the glasses in my kitchen. I love the assertiveness. I opened the door.

"Hey Megan, is everything okay with the car?" I asked. She smiled. "Yes, Bags, perfect. And I am pretty embarrassed that I didn't have it in park," she said.

I laughed. "We've all done it," I said.

"Are you gonna let me in?" she asked.

Although a rather attractive girl, she was about as timid as a charging rhino. "Of course, come on in," I replied. "Where are your boys?"

"They are working on pieces for their upcoming art show at school. They will be there for a couple hours, so I thought I would come hang out with you while I waited," she said. I told her I was glad she was here and that I just put some coffee on. I asked her what she has been up to lately.

"I've just been working a lot, and keeping up with the little monsters," she said. "I work as an administrative assistant at NECO Tools. They are an industrial distributor and I have known the owner's family for a long time, and they treat me well."

I couldn't imagine having that level of responsibility but now I understood where the assertiveness came from. It couldn't be easy for a girl of her stature to work in a male-dominated job like that. I am sure she has to be able to hold her own. I am also certain being a parent is more than I could handle, let alone a single parent. But she seemed to have it all under control, and although I had only had a few hours of interaction with her, I'd say she was doing a pretty good job bringing up those boys. They sure seemed well behaved to me. I heard the coffee finishing its brew cycle and went to get some for us. I couldn't remember how she took her coffee, so I fell on my sword and asked. "Megan, I am so sorry, but I can't remember how you like your coffee, can you remind me again?"

She turned to me with a look as if she was completely appalled. "Are you serious?" she demanded. "Bags, I am so utterly disappointed that you can't remember something as simple as how I take my coffee. How am I supposed to take this neighborly relationship seriously when you can't even have enough courtesy to retain the simplest of things?"

She has to be joking, I thought to myself. But the look on her face and her body language told me she was serious, and I was on my toes. She got up from the chair and began walking towards me. "Besides, I would expect you to at least remember that I poured my own coffee last time we got together. So you couldn't possibly remember...so you are lucky," she said with a vibrant smile.

I couldn't help but smile back, but I saw enough in that interaction to know not to cross her. She came into the kitchen to finish preparing her own coffee.

"I don't want to know how you make your coffee because I don't want that kind of responsibility," I said. She smiled and winked.

We sat down at the kitchen table and continued small talk. I asked her about Jimmy and Joey and what art projects they were doing, if they enjoyed art, and when their art show was taking place. She asked me about work, my relationship with Johnny, and how I know about cars. Just small talk. Like the last time, our interaction was very natural and comfortable. I enjoyed talking with her.

She started to flipping pages in my notepad and reading.

"Megan, what if the things I wrote in there were personal? What if I didn't want you to see that?" I asked.

She looked at me kind of sideways. "Then you would tell me to not look at it. Unless of course you are too weak to tell me what you're thinking. Besides, I'd have to have an interpreter or a hieroglyphics expert to read what you are writing here anyway. Dude, your writing is really bad," she said.

Wow, she was so straightforward, and I really liked it. I started to think I needed more people in my life to talk to me like this. It would probably help me.

"You're right," I replied. "I would tell you to put my notepad down before I do something I regret. And my handwriting isn't that bad. You can read it, go ahead and try." She then began to read it, but it was certainly not easy for her.

"That word looks like foundation, something your writing teacher never understood obviously. I see boat, fishing poles, rod holders...what is this? Joey, are you a fisherman?" she asked. I found it interesting she had called me Joey, as she had become very fond of referring to me as Bags.

"Well when you say it like that it almost sounds important. Yes, Miss Megan, I am a fisherman. It's a real passion of mine." She seemed to get excited.

"It must be in the name; my Joey loves fishing as well. My dad used to take him fishing until he got sick. He asks about it all the time. Maybe someday you can take him with you. He would love that," she said.

"Sure, I'd be happy to," I responded. But inside I was thinking I'd rather shove a hot spike in my eye then deal with tangled lines, hooks in fingers, whines of boredom, and everything else that comes with teaching a kid to fish. After all, I pretty much taught myself. But I am sure she read none of those thoughts, as I covered it well with a complacent smile.

She kept flipping through the pages. "Why are you writing this stuff down?" she eventually asked.

"Are you familiar with Father DeFalco from St. Joseph's Catholic Church?" I asked.

She was not, and quickly got defensive, saying that she wasn't religious.

"Neither am I," I said quickly, trying to ease her discomfort. "I have never been to the church, other than to deliver pizzas of course. But Father DeFalco is a close family friend of Johnny's, and he has volunteered to take me fishing with him. He is an amazing fisherman who holds several lake records and he has been meeting with me and asking me to write these things down so he can teach me his secrets. It may sound strange, but I am so excited about this I can hardly take it."

"That doesn't sound strange at all Bags," she replied. "I can tell you love to fish, and I'm sure you are excited to learn from someone like him. You will have to let me know what you learn."

"I will for sure." I replied. "So, what time do you have to be back at school?"

Megan glanced at the clock on my microwave. "Oh my, I am glad you said something! I better get going. Do you want to ride with me to pick up Jimmy and Joey?" she asked. As much as I would have loved to ride with her, I really wanted to get started scratching down some notes to define my target and strategy.

"Thanks for asking, but I want to work on something Father DeFalco asked me to do. But I would love to hang out with you and the boys again sometime," I told her.

"We'll hang out again Bags," she said as she walked out the door. "I am not very easy to get rid of. I'm kind of like a cockroach. I just keep coming back." I chuckled and said goodnight. She sure is the cutest cockroach I have ever seen, I thought to myself.

Target...now let's get to the target.

CHAPTER EIGHT

TARGET RICH

After Megan left to get her boys, and I was extraordinarily caffeinated, I was ready to get to work. The Father had asked me to scratch out my thoughts on a target and a strategy. This would be fun. First of all, father Defalco was clear by "target" he meant what kind of fish we would be going after. Since I knew he had held records in multiple species, I was confident I could learn something from him in whatever I chose. It was now March 17, and Father had said we would be fishing in two weeks, so I supposed I would consider spawning patterns in whatever species I chose as a target. I had always loved crappie fishing, and the story of that six-pounder that got away from Father DeFalco had me pretty excited to try our hand at that. In two weeks, it would nearly be April, but it had been a long winter, and slow to warm up.

Crappie spawn in the backs of creeks, and they migrate from the main body of water into the mouths of the creeks, moving in schools back upstream, and finally spawn in a few feet of water. As they move in from the main lake, they often suspend themselves under docks or over underwater structures. A single degree change of water temperature will cause them to move further back into the creek, and likewise if there is a cold front, they will move back towards the main lake. They are fun to catch, but difficult to find early in the season. I have spent many, many days searching for crappie that early, and unless Father DeFalco has some incredible secret to finding crappie, I am not sure I will want to start looking for them now.

Northern pike are early spawners. They typically migrate

to very small streams in late February or early March. Given that it had been colder than usual, they would be in spawn right about now. If I remembered right, they would start spawning when the water temperature warms to about forty-five degrees. I saw that the water at Mosquito Lake was forty-three, and I bet it is forty-five now given these few warm days. If they were on spawn right now, they wouldn't bite. Pre-spawn is always good, and post-spawn as well, but like most species of freshwater fish, they will not bite when they are in the middle of fertilizing eggs. Saltwater fish may be the same way, but I don't know much about saltwater species.

Therefore, I would consider fishing for northern pike because it would most likely be right after their spawn, and they should be very actively feeding at that time. I did catch a thirty-nine-inch northern a few years ago on a spinner bait while bass fishing. It was far from a lake record, but wow, what a fun fight trying to keep it from cutting my line with that mouth full of teeth. However, I did not have a great deal of tackle specific for northerns. I did have some casting spoons and bucktail jigs, but my tackle selection was limited. I wrote down northern pike as a possibility anyway. Next I considered walleye. I love fishing for walleye, and it is by far my favorite fish to eat. Walleye migrate into shallow water to spawn and prefer gravel or rocky bottom. Old roadbeds in creeks are common places to find these delectable fish. Walleye typically spawn at night and move out of deep water to come into the shallows to lay and fertilize their eggs. Walleye start their spawn when the water temperature is about forty-five degrees, just like northerns, but they spawn in completely different areas of the lake. In a couple of weeks, walleye could very likely be post-spawn and be very active. Most fish will stop feeding through their spawn, and walleye do as well. So basically, they slow or stop their eating for a week and deplete all their stored energy in the act of spawning. When they are finished, guess what happens. They eat and eat to refuel their bodies.

I know Father DeFalco has the lake record for walleye at Mosquito Lake, so I am certain he can share some incredible secrets. So that must be it. Starting in two weeks, we target walleye. Next, I have to think about strategy. I believed that what the Father was looking for was my suggestions on how we would approach our fishing trip. I believed he wanted to know my ideas about where we could find fish and what techniques we would use to catch them. Pre-spawn and during spawn, I have had great luck over the years jigging for walleyes with Sonar Jigs. When they are timid during spawn and have slowed their eating, I would often use a one-fourth-ounce curly-tail jig tipped with a minnow. I had been fairly successful catching walleye over the years, but I never seemed to catch big ones. Maybe this was what the Father would help me do. Post-spawn, I have had luck trolling for walleyes with deep diving crank baits or nightcrawler rigs trolled off of the bottom. I thought I would suggest to Father DeFalco that we start out trolling for walleye. We can cover more water this way, and if we don't find fish we can then see if they are still on their beds and try jigging.

There it was. I thought, I mean, we would definitely target walleye, and would likely start out trolling as our first strategy. I couldn't believe I was able to come up with what I thought was a solid target and strategy so quickly. It made me wonder if I had forgotten something, so I reviewed my notes, and felt pretty good about what I had come up with and the reasoning behind it. So, there it was, I had a target and a strategy, and I still had time to go through my tackle and get things organized. I spent the next hour or so organizing my lures and rigs to align with my strategy until I wore off the caffeine buzz and started to get sleepy. I realized I had not scheduled a follow-up with Father DeFalco, so I needed to reach out to him tomorrow and see when he wanted to get together next. I couldn't wait to meet with him again and tell him what I had come up with, but right now it was time to hit the sack and dream about getting on the water.

The next morning, I woke up at five thirty. Not sure why I was up so early because I did not have to be at the restaurant until ten o'clock. Nonetheless, all of those lessons of promptness from my dad left a habit in me that I could not break. When I wake up, I am awake. I rarely go back to sleep.

Inherently, I am full of thoughts. Sometimes my active thoughts do not inspire an active body, but that morning, I laid there for a few minutes trying to remember any of my dreams, but I could not recall anything, and within five minutes of awakening, my feet hit the ground.

I walked by the living room and realized I left a mess when

I was organizing my tacklebox and made a mental note that it would be my first task of the day to clean it up, but first I needed coffee. I made the coffee and sat at the kitchen table, thinking about my time with Megan the night before. It seemed like every little interaction we had made me feel more confident. I wasn't sure why, but maybe it was because our interactions always seemed to start with her having a request and I being able to help. We seemed to be on a similar wavelength, although we were clearly in different stages of life and responsibility. I couldn't imagine having the level of responsibility she had, but she seemed to face it head on, and from what I had seen so far, she was pretty good at it.

I finished two cups of coffee, reviewed my notepad, acknowledged Megan's observation that my writing is really bad, and got to cleaning up the mess I made in the living room. It was a Thursday, which is typically a slow day at the restaurant, but there was lots of work to do in order to prep for a busy weekend. It was now about 7:30 a.m. and I thought, I may as well jump in the shower and head in early, so I did just that. I often go in early, but I don't clock in until my shift. I don't mind giving a little extra at work because Johnny and his family have been so good to me. Selfishly, this morning I thought maybe if I went in early, I could catch Father DeFalco as he sometimes comes by around noon during the week. Johnny makes him and the kitchen staff homemade cinnamon rolls with our pizza dough that brings a smile to our faces. Nothing smells better in the morning than fresh cinnamon rolls baking in the pizza oven.

I finished showering, quickly got dressed and headed to the restaurant. As I left, I noticed that Megan's car was in her driveway. She must have the day off, I thought to myself. She could probably use a day off. I hoped that our paths would cross again soon.

I pulled into the rear parking lot. It was a great spring morning about fifty-five degrees, which felt like eighty degrees after the long winter. Young Tino was out back sitting on a bucket smoking a cigarette, which he quickly attempted to hide by throwing it under the bucket he was sitting on. He could not dissipate the smoke that obviously gave him away. He waved at me,

"Bags, you are here early," he said as I got out of my car.

"Yes Tino, just sitting around the house is not a recipe for progress, so I thought I could come help," I replied. "Those things are gonna kill you, and you can't hide from Mom and Dad forever," I added as I walked in the back door.

I entered into the smell of those amazing cinnamon rolls and had the suspicion that Father DeFalco had stopped by. I wished everyone a good morning and walked through the double doors to the front of the restaurant. Much to my dismay, I did not see the Father anywhere, and my face must have shown the disappointment.

"What happened Bags, did someone kick your dog?" Johnny yelled out from the front counter.

I chuckled. "No Johnny, you know I don't have a dog. Too much responsibility for old Bags," I answered. Johnny laughed and asked why I had such a look of disappointment. I thought to myself that my nickname is so fitting— I hide nothing. I told him that I was hoping Father DeFalco was here, and when I didn't see him... Johnny was smiling at me for some reason. I heard the bathroom door squeak as it opened behind me and out shuffled the old priest. He was smiling from ear to ear.

"Johnny you may want to wait a while to go in there. I just made a Holy mess out of the fragrance in your latrine," he said. Johnny chuckled and thanked him for the warning as the Father and I greeted each other.

Father DeFalco asked me how I was doing with my target and strategy and if I was ready to get started on the water. Johnny jumped into the middle of our interaction with some comment about a bromance brewing, and Father DeFalco chuckled again. "Johnny, how dare you. Besides, I might call it a spiritual bromance, just so no one gets the wrong idea," the Father said.

I loved this type of interaction and so did the two of them. I could tell already it was going to be a great day. The good Father asked if I had to start working right away and told him that I had actually come in early, so he asked me to join him for a cinnamon roll. I asked Johnny if he minded, even though I had an hour and a half before I was supposed to clock in.

"Who am I to step in the middle of a spiritual bromance? Of course, I will throw another cinnamon roll in the pizza oven," Johnny replied as he walked towards the double doors leading into the kitchen.

CHAPTER NINE

PERSONAL INTEREST

Father DeFalco and I went to sit at the table under the large window in the dining room. The good Father always sat at this table. I started to ask him why he always sits there and then I stopped myself. It really didn't matter, and I was excited to share my target and strategy with him.

"Well did you come up with a way for us to catch the next record?" Father DeFalco said as we sat down. I just chuckled, feeling a little odd, because I was hoping he was going to teach me how to break a lake record.

"Well, I have come up with a target and strategy, "I said, flipping over the coffee cup on the table. I still smelled those cinnamon rolls and I wiped my chin to make sure I was not drooling. "So, I think we should fish for walleye and we should start by trolling some deep diving crank baits," I continued. "If I'm thinking right, they should be getting off of their beds about now and will be starting to feed and chase more aggressively. We can cover more water this way, and if we don't hook up, we can get back over the roadbeds and try jigging to see if they are still on their beds."

I was so excited spitting those words out that it sounded like one big, run-on sentence, and I nearly ran out of breath before I got to the end. Then there was an odd moment of silence. Father DeFalco had his head in his hands. I must have been way off, I thought.

"I love it, let's do it!" the Father said suddenly, lifting his head out of his hands. We planned to hit the water the next morning.

I was so excited, I couldn't wait. It seemed like perfect timing, almost a congratulatory prize, when Johnny walked up to the table with those amazing cinnamon rolls. That smell! The sweet white icing...topped off with a fishing trip on the books. How could this get any better? Johnny dropped them off for the Father and I and said he had to run to the bank before we opened so he took off to do his business. We made probably ten minutes of discussion around the amazing cinnamon rolls, and then Father DeFalco asked me a question.

"So, what is going on in your life, Bags?" he asked. I didn't quite know how to take his question. I thought that maybe he thought I was up to no good or something.

"What do you mean?" I replied.

"I mean, what is going on in your life? You and I are getting to know each other, but we haven't talked much about anything other than fishing. I want to get to know the guy I am going to spend so much time with on the water," he said. I was excited to hear that he is already planning on fishing with me more than once. I better not screw this one up.

"Well Father there is not too much to this guy. I don't do a whole lot outside of work. I work, I go home, I watch TV, I do laundry, I wash dishes, I go to bed," I told him.

"That surprises me Bags. I thought for sure a handsome, smart, young guy like you would at least have a girlfriend," he said.

"Well I don't have a girlfriend, but I am becoming more and more intrigued with my next-door neighbor Megan," I said.

"Now we've got some things to talk about on the boat," he replied.

We continued to chat, and he continued to ask questions about me and my family, my upbringing, and other fairly personal subjects. I shared with him what happened to my parents and how I got laid off from my job but spared most of the detail. At one point he leaned in very close to my face and, honestly, I was a little weirded out. Then he suddenly took his napkin and wiped the icing off of my chin and he laughed and laughed. I really enjoyed being around Father DeFalco, he was full of life, had a great, old-school sense of humor, and was never in a bad mood, at least not that I had seen.

He began to talk to me about what I needed to do when I get home. He kept stressing that we had to be prepared for our trip in the morning. "Even if you don't get to sleep until really late tonight, you have to prepare when you get home. I will get the boat ready and will back my truck up next to the trailer. You will have to help me hook it onto the truck because these old arms aren't what they used to be," he said.

I told him no problem; I would be happy to. He instructed me to make sure that I ate in the morning, got new line on all of my rods, picked the crank baits I will be starting with, and make sure to have steel leaders. He also told me what he brings for lunch and suggested that I bring something similar. He told me to be sure to bring lots of stories, especially about this neighbor girl that he wanted to know more about.

I was intently listening and taking mental notes, because

I certainly did not want to disappoint. Father DeFalco asked if I had my notepad with me. I told him I had it, but it was in my coat pocket in the kitchen. "Well go get it, Bags! I have something important you need to write down." I quickly set down my coffee and headed to the kitchen.

On my way there I saw Tino. "What's up Bags? Are you becoming a priest?" he said in a typical Tino way.

"No Tino, I am confessing my sins. I can no longer live with the thought of the murder in my brain. I need the images to leave my mind, the blood, the screams," I said. I walked by him quickly and I didn't see his face and couldn't tell if he thought I was serious. I burst through the double doors to the kitchen, still smelling the cinnamon rolls and I went straight to coat rack. I got my notepad out of the coat pocket and walked back through the double doors. Tino looked a little rattled, still wondering if I was serious.

"I had to get my notepad; the priest is giving me some names of professional help. I need to write them down," I said as I walked by. Tino just nodded his head fearfully. I love to play these kinds of word games with the teenage boys. I always try to leave them guessing. I got back to the table with my notepad and Father DeFalco started immediately.

"Glad you brought your book because this is a good one and I am not sure it would be with me tomorrow," he said. "God gives me messages for people, and you are the lucky one today." His voice dropped to a whisper. "Your chance of success is directly proportionate to the amount of preparation applied," he said. He then repeated the message to me. He encouraged me to not forget the things he told me to write down.

"One day God may use these lessons to make you a wise man," he said. I wasn't sure how to respond to that. In fact, I was not even sure if there really was a God, or if He even knew who I was. Nonetheless, I nodded my head and broke off another piece of the cinnamon roll, which had cooled down and wasn't nearly as appealing as it was when Johnny first brought it to the table.

Much like the cinnamon roll, I thought Father DeFalco recognized that my comfort level had cooled as well. I am not sure why I was so uncomfortable any time the subject of God came up. I was certain the great nuggets of wisdom the Father had given me would add value to my life, I was just not sure what they had to do with God. In all the time I had spent as a student, I had learned that there always seems to be a right and a wrong answer. I couldn't get my head around something that I couldn't see, touch, hear, or experience in reality. I could tell when Father DeFalco mentioned God, it was not contrived, and he had a true belief. I found it interesting, but I was still far from understanding, or even wanting to understand.

We finished our conversation and understood that I was going on my first fishing trip of the spring the next morning, and my first fishing trip with Father DeFalco. I was looking forward to it a lot. I would have some preparation to do to get ready, and I didn't want to let the old man down. I would be prepared. Prepared to have a great day and to catch some fish.

Father DeFalco and I finished up that morning before Johnny got back from the bank. I couldn't imagine Johnny was taking that long just to do some transactions at the bank. I opened the door for Father DeFalco, and he shuffled out without looking back.

"See you in the morning Joey and be ready to catch some fish...God willing," he said.

"Oh, I will be ready...be at your house before sunup," I called back. The good Father shuffled across the parking lot and I went to start my day in the kitchen.

We had a good day at the restaurant and time went really fast. Sometimes I am amazed at my ability to do my job, no matter how fast paced, with my mind completely consumed with something else. By the end of the day, I had a very defined plan in my mind of the exact things I needed to prepare when I got home.

I told Johnny how excited I was to fish with Father DeFalco in the morning, and I could genuinely see the excitement he had for me. I ran to the grocery store when my shift ended to pick up some things for my lunch the next day. While I was there, I walked by an endcap and saw a display of chocolate soda. When I was younger, I used to always take chocolate soda with me on fishing trips, so I grabbed a six-pack and went home to get things prepared. The words "your chance of success is directly proportionate to the amount of preparation applied" rang loudly in my ears.

CHAPTER TEN

ON THE WATER

I set my alarm for 4:30 a.m. I read the time at 2:30, 3:37 and 4:12 before I finally shut off the alarm to keep it from going off. I would call that some serious anticipation. I just hoped that the morning coffee would keep me awake long enough to hook my first fish of the season. Once I hook that first fish, the adrenaline would take over and there will no longer be a sign of a lack of sleep.

I had packed my lunch the night before, so I was ready to go. All my rods were rigged and in my car. The only thing left to do was make some coffee, fill my little cooler with ice for the chocolate soda, and put some of that good-morning-go-juice in a thermos so I could partake while on the boat.

I also needed to get to Father DeFalco's house early that morning because I remember him saying he needed help. I was happy to do anything to help get us down the road. I finished the coffee, filled my gray thermos to the top, and locked the door behind me.

It was about sixty degrees that morning and my car came alive without too much coaxing. As I was warming the car up in my driveway, I noticed a light go on in Megan's side of the duplex. Boy she is up early, I thought to myself. Her front porch light turned on and she came out and stood there in her pajamas and slippers. I waved to her through the windshield and she lifted her hand and beckoned me over to her. I thought I must have been too loud this morning and I was going to get an earful from the little firecracker. I left the car running, opened the door and walked over to her and asked if everything was okay, in a quiet voice so the boys did not wake up.

"Yes, everything is okay, Joey," she said. Again, she chose to call me Joey out of nowhere. She then stood on her tiptoes and kissed me on my cheek. "I just wanted to wish you good luck today. I saw you loading everything up last night and even from a distance I could see the extraordinary gleam in your eyes. I heard you leaving this morning and I wanted you to know that I hope you catch the biggest fish in the lake," she said.

"Wow, Megan. Thank you. That's really awesome. I am going to do my best," I replied. She then went on her tiptoes again and kissed my other cheek. I told her I would stop over when I got back.

As I walked backed to my car, I was taken aback that someone, anyone, was paying attention to me, let alone this beautiful, little, independent woman who was starting to make me feel funny. She really recognized what this trip meant to me and that was pretty cool. She continued to stand on the front porch as I backed down the driveway, and I headed to Father DeFalco's place.

He lived about seven miles from my house, so it wouldn't take me long to get there. I was so excited. I had never been to Father DeFalco's house, but I have driven by it, so I knew exactly where I was going. As I got closer, my heart began to beat rapidly. I told myself it was probably the caffeine, but I knew there was more to it than that. At this pace I was probably going to pass out when I saw water. It was about a twenty-mile trip to the lake, so I would have plenty of time to calm down before the real excitement began.

I pulled into Father DeFalco's driveway at about 5:35 in the morning, and there was one light on in his kitchen. He had a split driveway that went around to the back of his house, and I could see the front of the truck nosing out from behind the garage. I pulled over to the right side of the driveway so we could make the turn with the boat. I grabbed my rods and walked around the corner to see the boat sitting there, ready to go. The man who gave me the nugget of wisdom about preparation had clearly followed his own advice. The boat was spotless, unbelievably organized, and appeared to be the machine of a walleye aficionado. Rod holders, remote trolling motor, a kicker 9.9 horsepower motor for slow trolling, a beautiful tangle proof net, and pretty much everything you would need to catch a giant. I thought to myself that Johnny's dad really set Father DeFalco up well.

I set my rods in the boat and noticed the rod holder on the opposite side had four open spots, so I walked to the other side, assuming that the Father had left those for me. At this point, I had not heard the Father moving, and assumed he would be out when he was ready. I walked around to the other side of the boat and secured my rods, and then I remembered that the Father had asked me to connect the trailer to the boat. I walked to the front of the boat. Father DeFalco was hiding there. He popped up suddenly and said, "Morning Bags!"

He just about made my heart stop, and I jerked back into a curled-up defense posture. The old man was cracking up.

"I just wanted to make sure you were awake and ready," he said.

"If I wasn't, I am now," I said.

We finished up getting everything ready and hit the road. The Father drove the truck to the lake and backed it down the ramp while I got it off the trailer. As usual, he planned every step long before it was time to take it. We got the boat launched. I got to drink an extra cup of coffee while I waited for the Father to come back from parking the truck, and we were ready to go. The Father reached down to start the motor and it started the first bump of the key, and I asked the old man where we were going to fish.

"Well, Mr. Joey, I heard your target and strategy loud and clear and I know just where to test it out," he said.

It was chilly. The sun was rising and left a beautiful orange glow across the lake. We were moving at about thirty-five miles per hour, and I was checking out all of the equipment. I couldn't believe the quality of his electronics. He had the best of the best. Everything from a full-color 3-D sonar, and even an old school flasher. There was no radio on the boat, and I asked Father DeFalco if he had one.

"What, a radio? That doesn't help you catch fish," he answered. I guess that was fair enough, I thought.

We headed to the southern part of the lake. When we were about three hundred yards from a large creek mouth, the old man pulled back on the throttle, tilted the big motor up, and dropped the small kicker motor in the water.

"Okay Bags, get the crank bait you are betting on and let's get to work," he said.

We both cast out our lines, and the good Father fired up the little kicker motor. It was really quiet. I noticed the Father was bowing his head and I assumed he was praying, so I sat quietly and let him. I have not been around many people in my life that openly prayed in front of other people.

We started to pull the baits and the Father began to tell me about where we are and why he chose this spot. He let me know about the roadbed on the lake floor that rises about fifteen feet on both sides. "If your strategy is right, it should happen right here," he said. We spent the next several hours running back and forth in different depths and adjusting our speed. The Father patiently taught me how to read the sonar. He could tell if there were fish there, what kind of fish, and how big they were. I started to catch on. Finally, the Father stopped the boat.

"Well Mr. Joey, what do you think is happening?" he asked.

"I really don't know, Father. I was so confident we were going to catch fish like this. Should we try another spot?" I said.

"Did you bring your notepad?" the Father asked.

"Father, why would I bring my notepad on a fishing boat?" He looked so disappointed before I continued. "That is what I asked myself before I put it in my coat this morning."

He chuckled at me. "Write this down funny guy," he said. He took a deep breath which I have learned by now is a dramatic pause used by a skilled speaker. "Never leave fish to try and find fish," he said in a dramatic fashion. "Write that down my friend. Never leave fish to try and find fish." I wrote it down.

"Let me explain that, Bags," he continued. "There is a power in this world that tries to distract us from doing great things. You may not see it, feel it, hear it but it is here. You felt very confident about your strategy, right?"

"Yes, I did," I replied.

"Then why would you want to change your strategy now? I showed you on the graph that there are plenty of fish here. Don't let the demons convince you that you are powerless. You had a strategy you were confident in. We have fish that we know are here. Do not let your belief waver now. You should be more confident now than ever. Tell me, Bags, what slight adjustments do you think we should make, because I am not leaving fish to try and find fish," he said.

What an interesting perception. My whole life, if I wasn't catching fish, I would just go to another spot. I pondered this for a moment. "If the fish are here, maybe it is our baits. Maybe we should try something else. All the fish you showed me looked like they were hanging very close to the bottom. Maybe we should pull a jig or spinner behind a walking singer to bounce it off of the rocks," I said.

"I love it!" the Father replied. He reached for his rod already rigged with a curly-tail jig behind a half-ounce wire walking sinker." It was like he already knew what I was going to say. I am not sure how because, I didn't know what I was going to say. Nonetheless, we were changing it up.

It was getting near 10:30 a.m. and the prime time for catching walleye was past us. I mentioned this to Father DeFalco, and he looked at me. "Good thing walleyes don't wear watches," he said. I think that was his way of saying that I think too much or maybe that I think of the reasons why things won't work instead of the reasons why they will. I wasn't sure if he was thinking that but if he was, he was probably right.

We started pulling the baits in the same spot we had spent hours at earlier. The first pull produced no results. We pulled up the lines to turn the boat and put them out again. About twenty-five yards into the second pull, my rod bent over mightily. At first, I thought I was hung up on the rocks, until I pulled the rod out of the holder and felt the tug and head jerk of the fish on the other end of the line. I fought the fish to the side of the boat and the old man was ready with the net like a pro. He scooped it into the boat without ever taking the boat off course. It was a nice eater walleye. Father DeFalco had a really good digital scale and I weighed it. Five pounds and twelve ounces, which any good fisherman would call a six-pounder. I threw it in the livewell and was ready to go again. Just then, the Father's rod took a hard dive towards the rear of the boat. Calmly, he put the boat in neutral and walked back to the rod holder. I reflected on what I did when my rod bent over. I nearly fell over rushing to my rod, while he was so calm. He removed the rod from the holder in one smooth action. I struggled wiggling mine out of the holder. He then calmly fought the fish, and I was by his side with the net. It was huge!

I was jumping out of my skin with excitement, while he was so calm. I reached in and picked the fish up by its gills and weighed it. Eight pounds and nine ounces— that's right, a nine-pounder. We landed two fish in about fifteen minutes.

Father shook my hand. "Never leave fish to try and find fish, Mr. Joey. Well done," he said. I couldn't believe it. The Father said we should stop for lunch and we nosed the boat onto shore to sit and talk about the action we had just seen. Our first trip of the year had already turned out to be the best trip I have ever had in my life. The Father and I continued to fish for the rest of the day but didn't catch anything else except a three-pound channel catfish that had decided to eat his jig. At the end of the day, I was emotionally spent. I was up and down all day long, yet I noticed that the Father was still as steady as they come.

We went back to the boat ramp where we pulled up to the dock. I jumped out to tie the boat up. As I looked down, I saw the Father with his head down again. I was quiet until he lifted his head up again.

"Well a pretty good day Bags, you have some fish to eat. I'll get the truck," he said. As he shuffled up the ramp, I watched him, thinking that he is the greatest man that ever lived. I couldn't wait to go again.

CHAPTER ELEVEN

SHARING THE CATCH

On the way home that evening, Father DeFalco told me that I could keep the two walleye that we took home.

"I would love that, but it is a lot of fish for just me to eat. Would you like to come over? I love to cook and can't wait to do my special beer batter for these beauties. I'll make some Carolina coleslaw, beer-battered fish and steak fries," I told him. My mouth was watering just thinking about it.

"Bags you forgot to tell me about your neighbor friend. I was so looking forward to hearing more. Maybe you should invite her over to enjoy the fish you caught," the old man said.

"You know, what Father? I think that's a great idea. Do you know she was standing on her front porch in her pajamas and slippers when I left this morning? She came out just to wish me good luck because she knew how important this trip was to me," I said.

"Oh my, Bags, that's not good. Any woman who pays that much attention to you can't be good. The next thing you know, she is going to be asking you how your day was and if she can help with anything. I would stop talking with her if I were you," he said. I looked at the old man, trying to tell if he was serious. He looked serious, but I didn't expect him to react like that. Then all of a sudden, he started laughing with that deep belly laugh he sometimes does.

"Well I hope she likes fish because it sounds like you need to fry up your catch for that girl," he said. I sat quietly for a while after his last comment. I thought he was right. It made me wonder why in the world it had taken me this long to recognize

Megan and pay any attention to her. I was going to go right over to her place as soon as I got back. I went on to tell Father DeFalco about Megan, and how inspired I am by her ability to raise such good boys by herself.

The whole trip back to Father DeFalco's, we discussed what we could have done differently to have better results. "Since it was our first time out, we could have built into our strategy to change up baits until we got them to bite. The reality is we didn't do anything wrong, Bags, we just didn't force ourselves to communicate," he said. I wasn't sure what he meant by that. It has been probably ten years since I have talked so much, so I asked him.

"Father, I am not sure I agree with you on that one. We talked consistently for a good three hours," I said.

He laughed. "You are right young man but get out your book and write this down. There are many reasons for communication, and I can't argue with you at all. We talked a lot and it was great. I really felt like I got to know you better and hopefully the same goes for you. That entire three hours of communication served a purpose which was to further our relationship. That is not a bad thing at all, but it did not enable us to impact our game plan. Write this down Joey– No strategy can be executed to the fullest without forcing yourself to communicate through the results. You see Joey, you have to constantly acknowledge where you are, what you are trying to achieve and measure your success with the results. If you are blessed to have a partner with you on your journey, you must force yourselves to communicate early and often to have the biggest impact on your results."

I wrote it all down. It was so simple. If you set out to do something, constantly acknowledge whether it is working or not, and adjust. It wasn't until the old man slowed the boat down and forced me to think about adjusting our strategy that we began to have better results. What would have happened if we had done that after the first hour of fishing? We may have landed even more big walleye.

As we rode back, I was flipping through my notepad, which at this point was a collective group of nuggets of wisdom with the potential to change the way I looked at things. Even my stubborn Italian mind could start to see the game changing a little. Although all these lessons have been about fishing, I felt like maybe Father DeFalco was starting to have an impact on how I thought about things. In fact, I couldn't wait to get home and ask Megan and the boys if they wanted to come over for dinner. This was entirely unlike me, but I was starting to feel like I had been holding myself back. As I read through the notes, I was reminded of the things he had taught me in that very short period of time, and I couldn't wait to see the changes that would happen after a few seasons of fishing together.

We pulled into Father DeFalco's driveway about five-thirty in the afternoon and the sun was high in the sky and it had warmed up nicely. The neighborhood dogs had knocked over the Father's trash can, and trash was spread all over his driveway. Father DeFalco grumbled something under his breath and I could tell he was a little frustrated. We pulled in and he parked the boat back where we got it. I stayed to help him clean the boat up and also to clean up his driveway as the old man told me about this pack of dogs that make it to his place about once a week.

When we finished up, Father DeFalco said he was going in the house to spend some time with the Lord. I wasn't sure if that was code for using the restroom, or maybe taking a nap. Nonetheless, we went our separate ways after a great day. The old man let me borrow his cooler so I could take the fish home, and I couldn't wait to share the news with Megan. In fact, I hoped they hadn't eaten yet, because I was ready to make a great meal and it would be a shame if I were to eat this meal alone.

As I pulled into my driveway, Megan and the boys were out in the front. Joey was riding his BMX bike, and Megan and Jimmy were playing catch with a small football. I could tell by the way Megan threw the ball that she was not new to sports. When I turned into the driveway, they all looked excited. In fact, Joey started riding his bike back towards his mom as if he just won the lottery. This made me feel like there was anticipation for my arrival, which I had not had in many years, in fact, maybe never. I pulled in, and the boys and their mom were all at my door and wanted a report.

"Well Joey, did you catch anything?" Megan asked.

I walked over to unlock the trunk and get the cooler out. "Of course I did, Megan, you know I had a strategy, and it worked... with a little adjustment," I said.

I asked Joey to help me get the cooler out of the trunk, and he couldn't drop his bike fast enough. I could see the excitement in his eyes. We set the cooler on the ground and he stepped back as I adjusted the carpet in my trunk. I turned around to see Joey and Jimmy both standing, waiting to see what was in the cooler.

"Well boys, what are you waiting for, open it up!" I said. Excited, the two boys opened the lid.

"Wow!" Joey shouted. "That's the biggest fish I have ever seen!"

I reached down and rubbed his head. "It's a good one, Joey. And I hope everyone's hungry because we are gonna clean 'em up and eat 'em. What do you think?" The boys began cheering and jumping up and down, and Megan had a gleam in her eye that told me they were in.

Joey and I carried the cooler to the side of my house where I kept my garden hose and an old two-by-eight board I have used to clean fish in the past. I asked Joey if he had ever cleaned fish before.

"No, but I used to watch my Grandpa do it," he said.

"Well, this time you are going to help if you want to," I said. I could tell he was excited.

We set the cooler down and I pulled out the board from under the plastic storage bin, wiping it with my hand and then set it back down. I told Joey that I would be right back and went inside to get my fillet knife. As I was walking inside, I heard Joey yelling to his mom that I was going to let him help clean the fish. I remembered how excited I would get about cleaning fish when

I was his age.

I came back out and Joey had already had the six-pounder out of the cooler and on the board ready to go. I loved the fact that he would jump right in, and it was not surprising given the nature of the little spitfire that has been raising this boy.

I normally liked to use a small five-inch fillet knife but that one would require me to get out the seven-inch knife that I hadn't used very much. I brought my sharpener and sat down on the ground next to Joey to show him how to sharpen the knife. I let him try to run it through the sharpener a few times. As I started to show Joey how we were going to cut fish, Megan and Jimmy came around the corner. I explained to Joey about cutting the fillets, and how important it is to make sure not to leave any bones. I took his hand and let him hold the knife as we did the first vertical cut right behind the pectoral fin, then sliced along the back next to the dorsal fin. I showed him how to find the rib cage and fillet around it to make sure there are no bones left in the fillet. Joey was attentive and took instruction well. I expected him to be nervous and unsteady, but that wasn't the case at all. He seemed confident and comfortable taking instruction from me. His brother just kept saying that it was gross.

We finished both fish and I let Jimmy and Joey take the scraps and put them far into the woods behind the duplex so the coyotes would eat them. The two boys ran off together, arguing over who would carry the bag of scraps. It was fun to watch. I finished cleaning up the mess and spraying everything off with the garden hose. I looked up to see Megan smiling brightly as if I had left my fly open or something. I looked down to make sure that wasn't the case.

"Why in the world are you smiling so big?" I asked her.

"Well Bags, I just think it's funny that I have been living next to this guy for quite some time and I had no idea what a great influence he could be for my boys. I mean I always thought you were kind of cute, but I would have never expected that," she said.

"Well let's not move too fast, I may not be the influence you want for your boys, but I enjoyed teaching Joey how to fillet fish. That's something my old neighbor taught me when I was a young boy, and I'm happy to teach him how to do that. I am going to take these fillets in the house and get started cooking. I am sure you'll want to clean Joey up before you guys come over for dinner, but just come whenever you're ready."

I went in and got the fillets soaking in buttermilk. That's another trick my neighbor taught me. The buttermilk helps clean the taste of the fillets, or as my neighbor would say, they taste less fishy.

I had a quick shower so that I could get busy on dinner, and man, I was getting hungry. When I was done, I began chopping cabbage for coleslaw, mixed up the beer batter, and slicing some potatoes. I heard a knock at the door. I yelled for them to come on in.

As the three of them kicked off their shoes, I heard Jimmy say to Megan, "Mom can you ask him? Please?"

"Jimmy, does your Mom have your lips? You can ask me anything you want," I said as they came in.

"Mr. Bags, can we play the video game?" he asked. I loved it. It sounded so formal when he called me "Mr. Bags."

"Absolutely, it is already set up for you. Have fun," I said.

The boys ran to the living room and I turned back to my stove. I felt a small hand on my side.

"How can I help you Mr. Fisherman?" Megan said.

"Well, at this point, Miss Megan, the only thing you could do is maybe get us all some drinks," She did so, and took the liberty of setting the table for the four of us to enjoy a great dinner together, and we did exactly that. What a great evening, great food, and great company. It was unbelievably comfortable. Young Joey had a different personality that I had not seen. He was full of energy, highly intelligent, and could hold a great conversation. Jimmy really looked up to his brother.

I kept thinking what an amazing job Megan has done with these boys. We all ate far too much, we laughed heartily and shared great stories. The boys got to tell their story about dumping the fish guts and thinking that they were being chased by a coyote. That was probably my fault.

At the end of the night, Megan wrapped her arms around me and pulled my ear down to her lips. "Don't tell anyone, but I'm starting to think I like the boy next door," she whispered. I blushed, kissed her on the cheek, and hugged her good night. Wow, what a day.

CHAPTER TWELVE

THE PLAN

The next few days went by quickly. Father DeFalco and I planned to get back on the water on my next day off, and I couldn't wait because that was the following day. The anticipation wasn't about the fact that I needed more fish, because I still had enough for another meal in the freezer. It's amazing how many meals you can get out of two big fish. It was really about getting back on the water with Father DeFalco and continuing to learn. It had been quite a few years since I had learned something new, and it was exciting. I am not sure if it was the fishing lessons, or the fact that his teachings seemed to somehow be all-encompassing. They seemed to be waking me up from the funk I had been in for years. I didn't quite have my finger on it yet, but I did know that when I was in the presence of the old man, I was in a good spot. The more I can be around him, the better.

In the last few days, Megan and I had very little interaction. We had waved to each other in passing, but it always seemed that when I got home from the restaurant, her lights were off and her and the boys were already in bed. She worked hard and keeping those two little ones occupied was a full-time job in itself. I kept thinking about her. I wanted to see her again, but it just hadn't worked out. After all, I kept thinking about her whispering in my ear that she was falling for the boy next-door and given the fact that I am the only one next-door to her, I needed to pay close attention. That is, of course, if I have any desire not to die a lonely old man.

As I headed into work that morning, I thought about

everything that was happening at the time and tried to get a handle on all of the events and new relationships. As I was thinking through it all, I couldn't believe how much Father DeFalco has invested in me. Our interactions seemed to be changing the way I think. I came to the conclusion that Megan and Father DeFalco were the two people that I should invest in. I had been working quite a few extra hours so I could probably afford to spend some of the cash I had saved up in my mason jars.

My thoughts quickly shifted as I pulled up to the back of the restaurant. Tino and a new hire Johnny recently brought on board were pushing each other as if an argument was about to escalate into a young, Italian boy brawl. When I pulled in it did not distract them at all, so I knew it was serious. I jumped out of my car and inserted myself into the middle of it.

"Guys, Guys, Guys– do this after work unless neither of you want to work here anymore" I yelled. The both looked at me, then turned their back on each other. Tino walked into the restaurant through the back doors. The new hire just got in his car and left.

I walked into the restaurant a few feet behind Tino, although my entrance did not mirror the aggressive stomp that Tino carried through the door. Johnny was already there, standing in front of the pizza oven, making more cinnamon rolls. I knew what that meant.

"Jeeze, Bags, what did you do to Tino?" he asked.

"I had nothing to do with it, you'll need to talk to him to see what's up," I replied. "But good morning friend, I could smell those cinnamon rolls as soon as I got out of my car. I take it Father DeFalco is in the house?"

"Good morning, and yes, the old man is sitting up front with my beautiful wife. I have to get out there because who knows what she is telling him about me," he said, and shrugged his shoulders just as I did. It was pretty obvious we spent a lot of time together.

As usual, I was thirty minutes early to work, so I walked through the double doors to greet both the Father and Dena, Johnny's wife. I hadn't seen Dena in quite some time, and she was smiling vibrantly as I walked toward the table. As I approached the table, Dena said, "And speak of the devil...there he is." It was obvious they were talking about me.

"Hello Dena, you look amazing as always," I greeted her. "But I have to ask, do you think it a good idea to speak of the devil in front of the good Father?"

She chuckled. "Oh, Bags, you know it is just an old saying. You know I love you and think highly of you," she said.

I turned to Father DeFalco. "Good morning Father. you look a little tired. Did Johnny not make your coffee this morning?" I asked.

"No, he made me coffee, but I was saving it to help me get the wallpaper off of my bathroom walls," he said.

I laughed. "I understand, I keep telling him to know his strengths, and making coffee is not one of his," I said. I asked the Father what special concoction he wanted from the Spirited Bean, and I would walk down and get him one.

"That's nice of you Bags, just tell them it's for me. They'll know what to do," he told me.

I turned to head towards the door and Dena asked if she could join me. I obliged and took the opportunity to catch up with her.

"So, Bags, Father DeFalco says you have a brewing relationship with a young lady?" she asked without hesitation.

I chuckled. "I thought priests were supposed to keep confessions to themselves and God," I said. We both laughed.

She told me how Father DeFalco was excited for me and how he really thought it could be good for me. I asked her if Johnny has been driving her crazy as usual, and her response was a definite yes. I always enjoyed their relationship because although they were brutally honest with each other, they clearly had a tremendous amount of love for each other and their kids. Dena went on and on about the kids as we got our coffee. It was obvious that she was completely consumed with all the activities, school, and sports. It seemed like a lot. I kept thinking to myself, what a strong woman she is and how similar she is to Megan.

We got our coffee and started back to the restaurant. "Dena," I asked, "if Johnny was going to do something to make you aware that you were on his mind, what would be the best thing he could do?"

She thought about it. "He could take one of these kids off my hands for a while. Seriously though, I always like it when Johnny sends me flowers. It shows me I am on his mind," she said. I said thanks.

"Oh boy somebody's gonna get flowers," she remarked, smiling from ear to ear. As we approached the doors to the restaurant Dena said she had to go meet with a guidance counselor and gave me a hug.

"Tell Father DeFalco goodbye for me!" she said as she walked to her car. I walked back into the restaurant to the smell of cinnamon rolls.

I gave Father DeFalco his coffee and confirmed we were still on for the morning. "Yes, we sure are, Bags. And this time, I want you to think through what we missed the last time. This time I want you to come in the morning with a plan," he told me.

"I am not sure I completely get it," I told him.

"Well Bags, so far I asked you to build a foundation which you did. I asked you to build a target, which you did. I asked you to build a strategy which you did. We then hit the water with those in place, but we didn't necessarily have a well-defined plan on how we execute and adjust our strategy to achieve success. This is the next step to success. Create a foundation, set a target, develop a strategy, and build a plan. "Tomorrow, I want a detailed plan for our trip, and of course I want to hear about your dinner," he said.

"You got it," I said. "I will be at your place at five o'clock with a plan. Right now, I have to get clocked in and get started making some red sauce. See you in the morning."

I walked back to the kitchen where Johnny was having an intense conversation with Tino, and I was sure I knew what that was about. I started getting my pots prepared to make red sauce and just let the conversation continue between the two of them. When Johnny was finished, he let Tino go home for the day, and he stepped in to help in the kitchen.

In a little while, he came up to me and asked if I knew what had happened. I told him that I saw them roughhousing as I pulled into the back parking lot and saw the other young man leave, but that was all I knew. It turned out that the new guy kissed Tino's girlfriend after work the other night, and someone saw it and told Tino. I knew there was something charging the testosterone and that makes sense.

"By the way," I said to Johnny, "you need to buy your wife flowers and take one of the kids off of her hands for a while. You're welcome." He didn't respond.

The day went blindingly fast, but I found time to take a thirty-minute break and go to the florist down the road. I went in to see an old high school friend working there. She was awesome and she helped me pick out some flowers for Megan.

"You know, Joey, all the girls had a crush on you in high school," she told me.

"Yeah right," I said.

She told me name after name of girls from school and things they had said about me. I didn't have a clue. The fact was, in high school I didn't have much interest in girls. I just wanted to fish every chance I got. There was a creek across the street in front of our high school and instead of prom or homecoming, I would go night fishing for catfish there. Nonetheless the stories built my confidence.

In describing Megan and talking to her about how Dena gave me the idea for flowers, she came up with a great idea. She said we should create a gift certificate to include in the flowers for one full day of babysitting one boy of choice. We had to say one boy because I wasn't confident in my ability to manage both of them. So, there it was, I bought her a beautiful bouquet of spring flowers and gave her an opportunity to hand off one of her boys for a whole day. I was hoping that would show her I was thinking about her.

That evening when I got home, I saw that no one was home at Megan's. I assumed she got the flowers, but I wasn't completely sure. If she has been gone all day, maybe she didn't. I had to get started with a plan for the next morning. I sat down with my notepad and the first thing I did was to write down the steps the Father told me earlier. Create a foundation, set a target, develop a strategy, and build a plan. After thinking about it, I believed that what he meant by a plan was defining all the steps to making sure your strategy works. I had what I thought was a well-defined strategy, but I did not have a plan to make sure the strategy was working. So, it has only been a week or so since we fished last and I still thought the target and strategy was a good one.

My plan came together. I would like to start our pulls in the morning with one rod on the starboard side of the boat with a crank bait, and one on the port side we would put a jig on a walking sinker tipped with a trailing night crawler. We would then pull along the roadbed four times before deciding to switch baits. If we got a fish on one of the baits, we would switch baits on both rods to match and continue to pull. I thought it was a good plan. I prepared my rods and got them loaded in the car and packed my lunch. It was time to get some sleep.

I slept well that night and woke up ready to go in the morning. I left the house at 4:40 a.m. and pulled into the Father's driveway at 4:55 a.m. I could see the old man walking around in the house, so I knew he was ready to go. I loaded my rods in the spots he left for me, connected the trailer, and as I was finishing connecting the trailer chains, Father walked out with a pep in his step. "What a beautiful morning, Bags. I hope you have a plan because I believe there are hungry fish waiting to be fed," he said.

"Well, Father, I think I have a good plan for us to try."

"Well, you aren't really confident in your plan are you Bags? Look in your book. Confidence comes with absence of thought. Do you think you have a good plan for us to try or do you know you have a good plan that will work? Choose your words wisely my friend," he said.

We hadn't even left the driveway yet and coach DeFalco was preparing me for victory. It was gonna be a great day.

CHAPTER THIRTEEN

ON THE WATER AGAIN

"Well Bags let's hear the plan," the Father said as we pulled out of the driveway. As usual, the old man got straight to the point. He knew I was a little confused about the difference between the strategy and the plan, so I really think he was ready to teach, and I was ready to learn.

"Well Father, I thought about it and I think...hold on let me start over. Well Father, I thought about and what we are going to do is begin like we did on the last trip. However, I'm going to put on a deep diving flat lip crank bait that we can pull slow. I will put that on the starboard side of the boat, and we should rig your walking sinker and jig combo on the port side. However, this time we should tip the jig with a night crawler," I said.

"I like it but is that your plan or an adjustment to your strategy?" he asked. I sat silent for a moment and so did he. He was so good at sitting quietly after a question. Almost like a skilled strategic salesperson or project manager. I suppose I am probably a project in his eyes.

"Well, I guess... I mean, well sir, that part is a slight adjustment to the strategy, but I wasn't totally done yet. We will make three or four pulls along the roadbed. If we are blessed enough to get a fish on one of the rods, we will stop and match the bait on the other side. So, we should start with two rods rigged to match each other's rigs. If we do not get any fish on the first pulls, we will stop and discuss what we are seeing on the graph and determine if we need to adjust our strategy. If we are catching fish, we stay with the strategy and execute the plan," I spit out as if I had thought it all out in detail. I guess I did, but when I heard myself say it, it all made sense. In fact, when I heard myself say, "if we are blessed enough." I think that may have been the first time I had ever used that phrase in a sentence. The old man is rubbing off on me.

Just as all this was happening, the Father turned onto the boat ramp. He turned to look at me and asked where I put the night crawlers. I said that I didn't get any night crawlers. He chuckled and began to turn the truck away from the boat ramp.

"Well Mr. Bags, let's go get some, we can't execute a plan without the necessary resources. Make sure you write that one in your book," he said.

"Well, I guess you are right, that was a miss on my part. I will go in and get them when we stop," I replied. Little did he know I had put my notepad in the storage spot in the side of the door when I got into the truck. I learned to be prepared for these things. I flipped it open to the last page had written in and began writing.

At this point, I was like a sponge. "There are four important needs in every good plan," he began. "You need people, resources, actions and a timeline. In order to have a plan that will succeed, your plan must address each of these. Ask yourself now, Bags, if your plan has all of these pieces before we get started."

I was writing furiously as we turned into the parking lot of the bait shop. This was great stuff. I started to ask the Father a question and he held up a hand to silence me.

"Bags, we have all day to discuss, but right now go get

some of the resources needed to execute your plan," he said.

"Fair enough," I said, and I jumped out of the truck to get the bait.

I went into the bait shop, found the cooler with the Canadian nightcrawlers, and picked up two containers of eighteen each. I noticed the man behind the counter waving at Father DeFalco through the window. I approached him to pay for the worms.

"Are you with Father DeFalco?" he asked me.

"Yes sir," I replied.

"What's the matter with the old man? Is he afraid he'd have to sign too many autographs if he came into the store?" he said. We both chuckled.

"Not sure, but I have gotten pretty good at his signature if you need me to sign something for you," he laughed again.

"That's alright, no one can take the place of that old man. You are lucky to be fishing with him today." I agreed and introduced myself as Joey to gentleman behind the counter. He greeted me with a hardy handshake.

"Nice to meet you Joey, you can call me Captain Mark," he said.

"Sounds good Captain Mark," I replied.

He asked me to say hello to the old priest for him and I obliged and headed back out to the truck. I jumped in the front seat.

"Let's hit it!" I said. "By the way, Captain Mark said to say hello," I told him.

The old man chuckled. "He is a good ole boy, and one day he will find the Lord." Once again, the Father has lost me, but I chuckled, and we headed back to the boat ramp.

As we pulled in, there was another boat docking and the gentleman in the boat waved to Father DeFalco. He seemed like the old man was a fishing celebrity. Like before, I jumped in the boat and he backed me down the ramp and I got an extra drink of coffee as he parked the truck. We were on the water in no time.

It was chilly again this morning moving across the water, but this time I was smart enough to dress a little differently. As we pulled into the mouth of the creek the old man pulled back on the throttle and we slowed down like a parachutist coming in for a landing. It was unbelievably smooth with a little push from the swell at the stern of the boat. The water was like glass. You would swear there wasn't any current. Knowing the structure of the lake and how the creek enters right here that isn't possible but that morning it was very still. Father DeFalco lowered the kicker motor and fired it up. The atmosphere was so still that the little kicker motor sounds louder this time, but I am certain it is because there wasn't a hint of wind anywhere.

We started the plan and I was so excited I could hardly think. I asked the good Father what he wanted to use first, the jig or the crank bait. I would give him choice but was hoping he would say crank bait because we caught them on the jig the last time. I had tied a white curly tail on a pink one-fourth-ounce lead head. Father DeFalco said that I could start with the jig and he would start with the deep diving crank bait. I looked over and noticed he was using one of my favorite crank baits, pink and white with a stripe of silver reflective tape down the side. He launched his bait out the side of the boat while I was finding the best worm to tip my jig. I was chuckling because I suddenly had the memory of fishing with my uncle when I was a little boy. He used to tell me that the worms would be the best if you put them in your mouth before you thread them on your hook. I never fell for it, but I always laughed.

I sent my rig out the side and as expected, the Father had a great line for us to follow. Before my line even hit the bottom, the graph was lit up with fish everywhere. "Well look at there Bags, looks like we found the bank now we just have to make a withdrawal," Father DeFalco said.

"Well, I think I know my pin number," I replied. At the exact time I said that, his rod bent over and the game was on. We didn't have our baits in the water for two minutes. I was not even sure mine had hit the bottom yet. Like before, he smoothly grabbed his rod and I got the net. We landed a nice little walleye and I turned around to see my rod bent over. I grabbed it without an ounce of the grace the Father had, and he kept the boat in motion and on the right line. I got the fish to the side of the boat. He was magically there with the net, and we pulled the second fish of the trip in the boat within the first five minutes. The Father kept the boat moving as I got them off the hook, weighed and in the live well. His fish weighed just under three pounds, and mine weighed two pounds and eleven ounces. Both of them just made the length limit and they were good eaters.

"Well, Bags, what does your plan say to do now? Both of us got a fish," Father said.

"Well Father, I didn't account for this, but I say we don't change anything– we have found the fish," I replied. The old man agreed, and we put our lines back out. We pulled the pattern twice after that and did not get a single bite.

As we pulled our lines up to turn around and make the next pull, the Father let out a grunt and I looked over to see him in a battle. His rod was buried. I quickly got my line in so I could help, and once again I could tell the fish was big, but he was in complete control. He fought this one for a while, wearing it out. With the net, I moved to the side of the boat he was on. The fish was getting close and it took off, stripping line off of his reel. We fished with eight-pound test, so he always coached me to make sure my drag would let him go if the fish wanted to run. He obviously had his drag set perfectly. It slowed again and he was able to get it to the side of the boat and it was bigger than the one from the last trip. I was shaking as I buried the net into the water to let the Father guide it into the net. I scooped it and lifted into the boat and high fived the old man. I seemed much more excited than he did.

I calmed down for a second taking a few deep breaths and I said, "That thing is huge! Do you think it is a new record?"

"Not quite, Bags, but that's a pretty fish. I'm going to guess nine pounds and three ounces," he said.

"No way, it's way bigger than that," I said as I was grabbing the scale. I lipped the fish with the claw on the scale and pulled it up. The digital read out was nine pounds and three ounces. That is when I realized that he has caught so many fish like this that he doesn't even need a scale. He was right on. What a fish! I can't imagine what his record breaker had to look like.

"Now do we switch our baits, Bags?" the Father asked.

"I didn't have it in my plan, but I can't let you catch all the big ones," I said. I went to my back-up rod, which was rigged with the exact same crank bait but a slightly different color. It was white and silver but had chartreuse highlights on the belly instead of pink. I was confident the color wouldn't make that much difference and I let it out the side of the boat as we started to pull again. On almost every pull, Father DeFalco would land a fish. He caught another one that was a little over seven pounds. I felt like a deck hand on a charter trip. I was netting and unhooking fish after fish, but they just wouldn't hit my line. I caught two small ones the rest of the day. The day was called short though, because we had hit our limit by noon. We couldn't keep any more fish. It was another amazing trip, although I didn't catch anything big, I certainly felt like I had helped.

We pulled the boat over to our lunch spot and got out the lunches we packed.

"Well, Bags, what do you think you would have changed this time?" the Father asked. I thought about it as I took a bite of my fried bologna sandwich.

"Well, I think I fell short in the resource area. I didn't have the right color bait, and because I did not have the right color, I didn't catch them."

"Yes, you definitely need the right resources and maybe this will give you a reason to go spend a little of that tip money on some pink and white baits," he said.

"For sure."

"It could easily have gone the other way and never forget we fish together as a team and we celebrate together as a team. Pick the fish you want to take home with you. And that reminds me, we didn't talk any more about Megan and her boys. We have to start the trip with that conversation next time. Put it in your plan."

I chuckled. "You bet I will, but if I am keeping fish, you are letting me cook some for you. In fact, if you do that, you can meet Megan and the boys yourself and give me your thoughts. I would like to hear your wise opinion," I said.

The Father smiled at me. "Maybe we can do that, Bags. Just maybe we can make that happen."

CHAPTER FOURTEEN

GREAT COMPANY

When we finished our lunch, we pulled up the kicker motor and decided to call it a day. As we headed across the water, I was thinking about the number of fish we had in the live well. Although I hadn't caught that many, and certainly no big ones, I was happy to be on the boat with the old man and to be a part of landing some really good fish. I had completely forgotten about the fact that I had sent Megan those flowers and wondered if she had received them yet.

I started to ask myself if I was moving too fast. I don't even know her story. How did she end up alone raising the boys? I realized that I would find all of that out when the time was right. The wind was blowing in my face as we moved across the water, and there wasn't any conversation during the twenty-minute boat ride back to the dock.

I was thinking about how I could get the old man, Megan, and the boys over for dinner tonight. I was going to work on him the whole way back to the house, and I bet I could make it happen. We pulled up to the dock and two boats were launching. Father DeFalco kept the boat out of their way and I told him to give me the keys so I could jump off the boat and go get the truck.

"Hey ya old fart, did you leave any fish in there for me?" one of the gentlemen launching his boat said to Father DeFalco.

"I left the small ones because I felt like you could handle them better. Get out of my way before I have to call on a higher power to split the waters and sweep you away," he shot back. Most of the times when Father DeFalco has an interaction like that, it feels rather comical and lighthearted. I noticed this time he wasn't smiling much, and I could sense some tension. Nonetheless, he backed out the boat and I continued my walk to get the truck. By the time I got the truck around, that guy had moved on and the Father was tied up to the dock waiting on me to back down the trailer. It was tricky and took me a few times, but eventually I backed it in, Father DeFalco drove the boat on the trailer, I secured the winch, and pulled it out of the water.

I pulled to the side so the Father could continue to organize the boat. I put on the stern tie downs and made sure everything was secure for the ride home. When I was at the back of the boat, I asked Father DeFalco about his interaction with that other man.

"It is not my job to judge people, Bags, I will leave that up to our Lord and Savior." He paused. "Good thing for him, cuz if it was up to me...oh boy," he added.

There was obviously a story there, but I wasn't going to pry any deeper. I was amazed at how Father Defalco handled himself in a situation like that. I was certain I would have handled it much differently.

As we got back in the truck, I asked the old man right away.

"So, can you come over for dinner tonight if I can get Megan and the boys to join us? I am going to make my special beer battered fish, Carolina coleslaw and some fresh fries. It would be award winning if anyone was giving out awards," I said.

Father DeFalco chuckled. "Well Bags, let's see if you can get the girl to participate and I just may do that."

"Awesome, I am going to hold you to it," I told him. "I hope

Megan and the boys are home when I get there. I sent Megan flowers the other day and I haven't talked to her since then. I am not even sure if she got them."

We continued to talk about Megan and the boys all the way back to the Father's house. The more I talked about them, the more I realized they were making a change in me.

We pulled into the Father's driveway and his trash cans were upright and stable this time. Another moment where we felt like we were winning. We backed the boat into its storage spot, split up the fish in the cooler (I took the small ones), and I headed back home. I had my notepad on the seat next to me and was looking at what I wrote down. At one point, I found myself swerving, and I closed the notepad and committed myself to spending some time with it this evening or tomorrow. As I rounded the corner onto my street, I genuinely became anxious to see Megan and the boys. As I got closer, I realized that her car was not there. I thought to myself that maybe they just ran to the store and they will be back. At least that is what I hoped.

I pulled in the driveway and popped my trunk. I first went inside to get my fillet knife, a garbage bag, and my knife sharpener and then went to the side of my house to get everything ready and set up. Without young Joey here, I was going to have to handle the cooler myself and I did just that, muscling it over to where I was going to clean the fish.

The last time we cleaned fish, I forgot to get a big bowl of water to drop the fillets in. I almost did it again, so I went back inside and grab the biggest plastic bowl I had. Then I went back out to the side of my house and got to work. I was moving through the fish pretty quickly when I heard a car enter the driveway. I looked around the corner, and it was Megan and the boys. Strangely enough, I got nervous. My heart started to pound a little harder. I heard the boys jumping out of the car and running in my direction, pushing each other out of the way to see who could get there first. They were both out of breath when they got near me.

"Awesome Sauce!" Joey screamed out, and I chuckled.

"Did you catch any big ones Mr. Bags?" I laughed because that "Mr. Bags" thing never gets old. I love it.

"Well Joey Father DeFalco and I caught two really big ones and all of these good eater size fish," I said. "We had a great day. I will show you some pictures later on. Father DeFalco kept the big ones and he is cleaning those."

Then Joey asked a funny question. "Do you fish with your Dad?"

"No Joey, I don't. My Dad is no longer around. He passed away," I said, perplexed.

He looked very confused. "Then why do you call him Father?" he said.

"Well Joey," I explained with a chuckle, "people call him that out of respect for his position at the church. He's a priest."

He asked a few more questions, some that I didn't quite no how to answer. For example, he asked, "Why is he a Priest?" I had nothing. Joey continued to look confused.

"Well I hope your Mom and..."

Just as that came out of my mouth, Megan came around the corner and she looked stunning. She had a dress on. which wasn't the norm for her, and her hair was down which was out of the ordinary as well. I stood up as she rounded the corner and I had my hands out in front of me covered in fish slime and blood.

"Hello Miss Megan, don't you look beautiful. Unfortunately, I am not in a position to hug you but let it be known the desire is there," I said. She smiled and stepped in closer to me, and I put my nasty fish-covered hands further out to my sides. She reached up to my face and wiped something off of my cheek. I assumed it was a fish scale or something. She attempted to remove it from my face three times before I leaned forward so she could reach it better. As I bent over, she reached up and put both hands on my cheeks and planted a great big kiss on my lips.

"Thank you for the flowers. It has been a long time since anyone has done anything like that for me. It made me feel really special," she said.

"Your welcome," I replied. A great interaction, no matter how awkward it may have been with slimy fish hands.

I looked down to see the boys throwing all the fish scraps in a plastic bag. I am sure they want to feed the coyotes again. There were two fish left and I asked Joey if he thought he could clean one by himself

"I think so, Mr. Bags. Can I try?" he said.

"Absolutely, but before you make the cut, I want you to tell me what you are going to do so I can tell you if you are doing it right. But before you start, let me go wash my hands so I can hug your Mom," I said.

I ran in the house and Megan followed me. I washed all the guts off my hands with this hand cleaner I get through the distributor at work that helps remove all the smells. I turned around to find Megan right behind me. I hugged her gently and she laid her head softly onto my chest. We stood there for what felt like 20 minutes, but I am sure it was really 20 seconds.

"I AM falling for the guy next door," she said. I kissed her gently on her forehead.

"Let's get back to Joey before he cuts his finger off. Oh yeah, can you come over for a fish dinner again tonight? I have a special guest." I asked.

"Absolutely," she said.

As I walked closer to Joey, I realized he was going through the steps, saying them out loud to himself. He is a thinker and I can relate to that. I walked up and Joey was ready. He repeated all the steps flawlessly and needed very little guidance from me at all. He did a really nice job cleaning the fish. Of course, he left some meat and a few bones in the fillets, but all in all he did a really nice job. He finished up and threw the last fillet in the bowl and he and Jimmy ran into the woods to throw out the scraps. I told Megan, I was going to head in, shower and get ready to cook. I asked her if six o'clock would be good, and she said that would be fine, and kissed me on the cheek as I turned with the bowl of fillets to head in the door.

I walked in, set the bowl down, and called Father DeFalco

and asked him if he could be there by six o'clock. He said he would check with God and asked me to hold on. He then came back on the phone and said, "My Father said it is okay." Once again, we both chuckled, and he asked if he could bring anything. I told him he could bring something if he wanted. I hung up the phone, soaked the fillets in buttermilk and jumped in the shower.

After cleaning up I started cooking and promptly at six o'clock, the doorbell rang. I opened the door to see Joey by himself. I opened the screen door.

"What's up, little man, where is everybody else?" I asked.

"They are coming, Jimmy was giving Mom a hard time," he said. Just then I looked up and saw the old man's truck pulling in the driveway. I let Joey in and kept the inside door open so Father DeFalco could see us inside. Father DeFalco parked his truck and shuffled to the front door where he ignored the doorbell and knocked lightly on the plexiglass. I opened the door for him and welcomed him.

Joey was standing in the kitchen with me. "So, who do we have here?" the old man asked.

"My name is Joey," Joey said, and stuck his hand out to shake. I was impressed.

"Father, this is Joey, and he helped me clean the fish today. Actually, he cleaned two of him all by himself," I said. When I said that, I saw the confidence grow in Joey's body language.

"Wow Joey that is impressive. After we eat, I will show you some cool fish pictures," Father DeFalco replied. He handed me a bottle of white wine and said he thought this would go good with the walleye you caught. I took the wine and snickered because the old man had caught most of them.

I turned and set the wine on the counter and heard Megan and Jimmy entering the door. Megan was still in her dress and still looked stunning. I greeted her with a hug and little Jimmy had a smug look on his face. I bent down to his level.

"Little man there is no reason to be grumpy, your Mama loves you and we are gonna eat some fish and if you start smiling, I may let you play video games," I told him quietly.

He immediately smiled. "That a boy," I said. Megan introduced herself to Father DeFalco. "Hello sir, my name is Megan, and these are my boys Joey and Jimmy. I am the annoying neighbor girl."

Father DeFalco chuckled. "I am not sure how a pretty girl like yourself can be much of an annoyance. I am Father DeFalco and it is a pleasure to meet you," he said. I could tell this was going to be a great night.

"Okay everybody," I announced, "the food is ready, let's sit down and eat before it gets cold." Everyone sat down to the table which I had already set, and Megan jumped up and asked everyone what they wanted to drink and took charge. I told her Father DeFalco brought us some wine, so she poured all three of us a glass.

We all sat at the table and the old man asked if he could bless the food.

"Sure, Father," I said. He reached out to take my hand and

we all joined hands and the Father bowed his head and began praying.

"Lord, thank you for allowing us to spend this wonderful evening together, thank you for hanging the sun, breathing the clouds into existence, and giving us all the ability to enjoy them another day. Father, thank you for giving Bags and I time together on the water today and for blessing us with this catch. Please bless the hands that prepared this food as we give thanks to your son Jesus Christ for fueling our bodies to praise His name. Amen."

Everyone lifted their head and immediately reached for the food in the Center of the table. We all ate until we were ready to pop. Right after we ate, Jimmy went to the living room to play video games, but Joey was mesmerized by Father DeFalco and he sat next to him and hung on every word. Megan and Father DeFalco hit it off really well, realizing that they had a similar sarcastic sense of humor. All night they played off each other, almost finishing each other's thoughts. Then the Father remembered he told Joey he would show him some pictures. He pulled out his wallet full of small wallet size pictures.

The old man pulled Joey onto his lap, which was not easy because Joey wasn't a tiny little boy anymore. He went on, one by one, explaining exactly what the weather was like, the water temperature, the color of the water, the bait he had used, and more, about every worthy fish he had in his wallet. Like me, Joey hung on the Father's every word. In fact, fifteen minutes into this, I realized Megan and I were both mesmerized as well. This continued for quite a while.

Joey asked tons of questions and the old man was always patient with him, filling his little brain with so much knowledge. Then Megan noticed little Jimmy passed out on my ottoman, with the game controller still in his hand.

"Excuse me, Bags, but I need to get him home. He's a tired boy. I had an amazing time. It was an unbelievable pleasure meeting you Father DeFalco. Now I understand Bag's infatuation with you, clearly a man crush," Megan said, and they both laughed. She wandered into the living room, pried the controller out of Jimmy's hands, and Megan scooped him up like a sack of potatoes.

We all said our goodbyes and Megan, Jimmy and Joey headed out first after a kiss on the cheek for both the Father and me. The Father shuffled out behind them and as he walked by me holding the door.

"Bags, write this down in your book. Never question an opportunity so much that you don't take action and lose the opportunity. You don't want to lose this one, the whole thing is beautiful. Good night my friend," the Father said.

"Good night, Father DeFalco, and thank you."

"Thanks for what? Telling you what you already know? Don't let this fish get away...you will never forget it."

CHAPTER FIFTEEN

INVESTMENT REWARDS

The next morning, I woke up thinking about a dream I had. It was a strange dream like they can be sometimes. I dreamt that I was on a boat with Father DeFalco and Megan's little man Joey. It was definitely Joey and he looked like himself, except he had a full beard and had a fillet knife strapped to his hip. The dream started with Father DeFalco praying, and as soon as he said amen, his rod hit the water. Oddly enough, in the dream I was fishing with what looked like an ice fishing pole, or a Mickey Mouse rod. It was a tiny little rod like I was a little kid or something.

Father DeFalco had four or five rods fanned out in front him. He fought the fish he had hooked with multiple grunts like he did with that big one we caught the last trip. He pulled the first fish up, I netted it and brought in the boat, and immediately another one of his rods bent over. I unhooked the fish and Joey filleted it in about fifteen seconds. This went on for a while. Fish after fish after fish, until all of a sudden, my little rod bent over and it had a huge fish on the line. I fought it by myself for what seem like forever. Father DeFalco kept catching fish after fish and Joey was the fillet master. There was a two-foot pile of fillets in the back of the boat. I struggled with my fish and at one point, I thought it was tired out and it would go running and stripping line off of my kiddie pole. This happened three times and then, somehow, the fish got stuck under the boat.

I had Joey hold my rod as I leaned over the boat and put my head under the water to see Megan's face with a hook in her lip staring right back at me. At that moment I heard a plop in the water and she, or it, swam off. I pulled my head out of the water with a look of horror. Little Joey was now clean shaven and looked like a little boy. "I'm sorry, Mr. Bags, I didn't want her to get away," he said.

Then Father DeFalco spoke without even looking at us. "Well I guess someone else is gonna catch them a good one," he said. Then I woke up.

It wasn't hard to decipher the message I was supposed to get out of that. I attributed the whole thing to the comment Father DeFalco made to me as he left last night.

"Don't let this one get away."

I kept trying to think of the exact words the old man had told me to write down in my book, but all I kept thinking about was him saying, "don't let this one get away." I agreed with him. I couldn't believe someone as amazing as Megan had any interest in me. I certainly didn't want to blow this one but if I was a betting man, I would find a way to screw this up.

Then, I remember what he said. "Don't think about an opportunity so long that by the time you act there is no more opportunity." It was something close to that. Once again, I found myself flipping through the little book for wisdom that I had gathered from my short relationship with the Father. I couldn't imagine what it will be like a couple years from now. I would have enough wisdom to run for President, or maybe too much wisdom to run for President. I guess that is yet to be seen. I looked forward to the ongoing journey with Father DeFalco and can't but help to think I have two new relationships I can't afford to screw up, although I had a history of doing just that.

It seemed as if time was moving really fast. The next few months seemed to fly by, and things just seemed to be so perfect, it was blowing my mind. Megan and I continued to learn about each other, and my relationship continued to grow with Father DeFalco. In fact, I found out why Megan was single because I finally got up the nerve to ask. It seems she was married very young and her husband was in the military and was unfortunately killed while stationed in Iraq. It was an intense emotional conversation. When she began to shed tears, I realized how much it still really hurt her.

It was probably good that we were moving at a slow pace. One reason was because she needed time to heal before she could completely fall in love again, and secondly, I needed time to understand everything, so I wouldn't go off and screw something up. Megan said that Joey had a solid memory of his dad, but Jimmy not so much. He picked up on things Joey said and made them his own, but he was very young when it all happened. It was tough to have this conversation with Megan, but I think it was good for both of us.

Over the next few months the Father and I fished together at least once a week and he continued to help me through the growing relationship with Megan and the boys. He continued to breathe wisdom into my thought process that didn't exist, not even in the smallest state, prior to our relationship. It seemed as if the old man was put in my life for a reason, almost unexplainably.

When I thought about all of the things that had to line up

properly for us to start fishing together, it made me question whether it was happenstance or if there was a greater plan that was being played out. As much as it didn't make sense to me, it almost seemed impossible to just happen. It can go as far back as me losing my job in the downsizing and then Johnny saving me after I made a really stupid decision.

Then Scott moved away without me knowing, and I overheard the conversation between Johnny and Father DeFalco. I met Megan at the same time that I was building a relationship with the old man which helped me open my heart for her and the boys. This just all seems incredibly coincidental or maybe what the Father says about a greater plan is true.

One thing I wrote in my notebook that I will never forget but can't say I completely understand was when the Father said, "No matter how well you prepare, strategize, or plan, if it is not God's will, it will not work. So constantly seek His will."

I will never forget it because on one of our trips the old man must have said it thirty times. I was about ready to push him out of the boat. At one point I reminded him that I was much younger and stronger than him and I could push him over.

"Go ahead, Bags," he said, "but just remember that one day you will have to answer to someone for your actions. Choose wisely. You can write that one down too." I laughed but I did write it down.

I filled pages and pages of these nuggets of wisdom and he coached me all season long on the steps. Foundation first, target second, strategy third, plan fourth and the last step is to execute. He drove home the fact that you have to be prepared and in fact he called me out a few times when I got lazy and didn't have rods in rod holders or didn't really have a plan. I felt at times that he was exaggerating all of this, but in a way that would make it clear what was important to be a successful fisherman.

It became clear to me that I was also connecting these lessons to the other areas of my life and realizing that this kind of thought was a big part of what I was missing. Through all of this, he also drove home the point that oftentimes, you have to adjust your plan or strategy to achieve better results. One of the notes that came from the old man was when he said, "You put a lot of hard work to prepare, build a foundation, identify a target, set a strategy, and build a plan. Then you execute it, but it doesn't show results, none of that effort was wasted, you simply identify the area that needs adjusting, and adjust." I found myself using this when we fished, and with my relationship with Megan. I also applied some of these lessons to my job at the pizza shop and found myself improving things that have been done the same way for years that never really made sense.

Once, Johnny walked by me after I reorganized the supply shelves in the kitchen. "I see Father DeFalco is making an impact on you," he had said. I didn't reply, but it caused me to look inward and recognize that he was probably right. After being around the old man a while, I was changing. I was being more intentional. My confidence was growing, and I had actually started to question what I was doing working in a pizza shop.

Father DeFalco was making an impact on me, and I liked it.

As the season progressed, one thing stayed very constant. I followed Father DeFalco's lead in building our strategy and plan, and he followed my lead to execute. Trip after trip, he would out-fish me. Almost every trip he landed a fish that weighted more than eight pounds, and I caught very few over five pounds. I decided what we would fish for, what baits we would use, and how we would fish for them, but he continually caught twice as many fish than me and caught all the big ones. As frustrating as it was, I was still thankful that I had such a great mentor to learn from, and I was incredibly thankful for the mindset change he was creating in me.

"We fish together, we celebrate together," he would always tell me. I never felt slighted, yet I would always wonder what kind of magic potion he was putting on his bait.

"Father DeFalco, you and I do the exact same thing. The same baits, the same method, the same everything. How do you catch twice as many fish as me?" I asked the old man several times.

"Well Mr. Bags maybe you are not holding your pinky right," he chuckled. "Just keep doing what you are doing, and it will happen. Remember, one fish changes everything. You may be saying to yourself; these trips are just not panning out for me. Then, that fifteen-pounder gets hooked, and you forget about all the ones you didn't catch. That one fish changes everything."

He didn't tell me to, but I wrote that one down in my book as well. It was very profound, and he was absolutely right. About midway through the season I began to watch Father DeFalco intently to see if there was something that he was doing that I wasn't. I began to match my entire routine to what he was doing, and it still didn't change anything.

As I continued to mimic his every move, I realized the only thing I wasn't doing was praying like Father DeFalco did before and after the trip. At one point, I closed my eyes and bowed my head, but I was just thinking to myself, what is he saying? It felt really awkward and I didn't do it again. That was just not going to be a part of my routine.

"What are you saying when you talk to God?" I asked him once.

"I am just thanking Him for this day and the opportunity to enjoy what he has created and asking Him to keep us safe as we go catch some fish," he said.

"Cool," I said, thinking to myself that would never happen with me. I would leave that part to the old priest. I can't seem to bring myself to talk to something I can't see, and frankly, am not convinced is real. I know millions of people can relate to the Father, and are perfectly fine praying, but I guess I am just not there yet.

We had a great summer together and were heading into fall. If you would have told me last winter that I was going to become best friends with an old priest and he was going to change the person I am, I would have scoffed at you. In fact, I may have told you that you are crazy and not given it a second thought. But, in truth, that is exactly what has happened. I am so glad Johnny asked Father DeFalco about his records in the kitchen that day, it has changed my life.

The old man always said, "You will be rewarded when you invest in others." You can tell that he really believed it. He couldn't hide the passion in his words, and no matter the words he chose to make this point, it was clear. He always thought of himself last and others first. Maybe that is what made the good Father so special. I am not sure, but I couldn't be more thankful than to have spent the summer fishing with him and was looking forward to the fall season. Maybe my luck would change, and I would start landing some big ones.

CHAPTER SIXTEEN

NOT AT HOME

Fall was setting in and the weather started to turn. The air was beginning to cool and the leaves starting to change slightly. It was September 29, to be exact. The Father and I fished often that season. But the old man had been feeling a little under the weather the last few weeks, and he wasn't up to getting on the water. He said he had a bad head cold and just couldn't muster the strength to get moving.

I understood completely because when I am under the weather, I am tough to handle and really can't get my feet under me. My dad used to always tell me to suck it up, while my mom would baby me. She used to make the best chicken soup, and she made dumplings that she put in it that she called "ribbles." They were nothing more than flour dumplings cooked in warm chicken broth, but they were so satisfying, and always made me feel better. Even though I never really learned my mom's recipes exactly, I spent enough time in the kitchen with her that I could make most of the meals she would and get them to taste pretty close to how she did it.

The next week I stopped at the store on my way to the pizza shop and got everything I needed to make the soup. I arrived early, before the first shift, and made a batch for Father DeFalco. My mom used fresh carrots, celery, fresh chicken (mostly dark meat from thighs), and lots of chicken broth. She would spice it up with salt, pepper, and bay leaves, and of course the "ribbles."

I swung by Father DeFalco's on the way home, dropped it on his porch, rang his doorbell and left. I left a little note that said, "This is how my mom always made me feel better. Enjoy!"

He made it to the door before I got out of the driveway. I waved to him, and he waved back. He definitely looked like he was battling something, but he was not moving too badly, and I was certain the soup would lift his spirits. That was on a Sunday.

He called me on my day off on Monday, and thanked me for the soup, and went on and on about the dumplings. There is something about those simple balls of flour that never fail to excite. He said he was starting to turn the corner and asked if I was up for getting on the water Saturday. It so happened that I had the afternoon shift at Prezioso's, so I told him I could fish early, but would need to get off the water before noon. He said that worked perfectly because he had Saturday Mass and really shouldn't miss another one. We were about to get back to action! Before I got off the phone with him, he was sure to talk to me about my preparation.

"It has been a few weeks since we have been on the water," he said. "Can you look at the water temperature and be certain to change our strategy and plan to increase our chances of limiting out? You have done well all season but pay close attention to the change in weather."

"You can count on me," I replied.

"I know I can, Bags, for more than just fishing. You are a good man," he said. That made me feel really good, and I started to realize that it was comments like that, that really motivated me to be my best.

Some people are motivated by fear. Some people are motivated by money. I started to realize after all these years that

I was motivated by praise. This probably explained why I had been with Johnny for so long, because he respected my opinion, and always praised me, which is what kept me driving to perform better. I am sure if I went a level deeper, there was a reason for all of that, but at that point, I was happy that I recognized this and had an idea of what motivated me. Kind of like the chance of catching the biggest fish in the lake and getting to fish with most amazing man in the world. I couldn't wait for Saturday.

That week at the restaurant was an interesting one. Johnny was a handful to most everyone at the restaurant. He is never like that with me. I think it was, in part, because I was his confidant, and he knew he can trust me to discuss what was really driving his change in behavior. He shared some frustration and challenges he had been having at home. A slight financial crisis he had gotten himself into created quite a bit of pressure. He had lots of assets, so he could probably sell himself out of the crisis but convincing his family to let go of some things proved challenging. I was happy Johnny could share this with me, and when he jumped down the throat of one of the staff, I always stepped in.

"Don't worry. It's not you. Johnny is under a little pressure right now and you are catching the brunt of his stress. We should just work hard and show him we are thankful, and we are here to support him," I would tell them. For the older staff, this always seems to calm them down, and created a more focused approach to what they were doing. To the young staff, it tended to be followed with a reply of several cuss words and all the reasons why they don't need this job. Funny the difference a few years and more life experiences can make. Johnny and I had several conversations that week that he asked me to keep to myself. He knew he could always count on me for that.

Friday night was crazy at the restaurant and I did not get out the door until 10:30 p.m. which meant I got home at 11:00, and I had to be up at 4:30 a.m. to get to the old man's house and get on the water. I had worked hard on a new strategy. I researched water temperature and read multiple fishing reports and realized there has been a change in activity. I had a good plan put together and couldn't wait to walk Father DeFalco through it in the morning. According to the fishing reports, the fish are getting really active as the water temperature continued to cool and I thought that early morning was going to show our best results, so I wanted to make sure I got the boat hooked up early and got out the door. I was sure the old man would be thinking the same thing and if I knew him, he would have done the extra work, no matter how hard, to get the boat hooked onto the truck so we could just pull out of the driveway when I got there. I was sure Father DeFalco hadn't completely relied on me to do the research. I am sure he had done some himself, and we would see if he had the same thoughts.

Because I had gotten home late that night, Megan and the boys had already been in bed. All the lights were off, and I had learned to respect Megan when she was tired. As sweet as she can be ninety-eight percent of the time, when she is tired, she gets this little flare behind her ears that makes me think she is part king cobra and could strike at any moment. However, I did tear a page out of my notepad and wrote a note and put it on her door. I didn't get a chance to tell her that Father DeFalco was back in action and we are fishing in the morning, so I wanted her to know.

It felt like I slept for thirty minutes, and my alarm went off at four-fifteen in the morning, because I set it early to get out the door. I also set the coffee pot to brew early, and I can smell the aroma coming from the kitchen. I had everything ready to go. I filled my thermos, put a hat on my head and walked out the front door. Yes, I did sleep in my clothes, and admit I get as excited as a child when it comes to fishing.

As I pulled into Father DeFalco's place, there were no lights on, and the truck was not backed up to the boat. In fact, it was still sitting on the opposite side of the driveway. I was disappointed, and I couldn't wait to have the conversation with him about being prepared. This could be fun. I would wait until I saw some lights come on, and I would get the keys off of him as he got ready to go. If he is like I am, it will take him a while to start moving full speed again after being sick.

I got my rods and the nightcrawlers out of the car and I walked around to where the Father has a motion light over the boat that shines right into the center. I used to think he did that for security reasons, but I now realize it was a strategic move to be able to load the boat hands-free in the dark.

As I walked around the boat, the light came on and I loaded the rods in the rod holder. I looked over at the old man's number one rod and he had the same bait on as he had on the last time we fished, which was about three weeks ago. He was either testing me and wanted to see what kind of plan I brought without any hints, or again, he was not very prepared, and if that were the case, I would match his sarcasm during this trip. I figured once the light came on it would only be a short period of time before the Father would get moving.

I looked in the window and saw he hadn't even set his coffee pot to brew. Boy, he is off his game, I thought, but I guess I could let it slide for once. No way, this was going to be fun. He had my soup bowl on his counter all washed and ready to give back to me, so he wasn't totally disconnected.

I patiently waited for the next fifteen minutes and no movement. So, I went to the door that entered into his kitchen and knocked and knocked again. I tried to turn the doorknob, but it was locked so I knocked once more. I was not sure where his bedroom was, so I thought he might not be able to hear me knock on the door. I went around to the front door. I knocked, but there was no movement. I rang the doorbell, and rang it again, and now I was really worried. Did something happen? This is one of those moments where a cell phone would come in really handy, but I didn't have that option, so I ran back to the old cutlass and raced back to my house.

I pulled in the driveway and the lights were still off at Megan's, so I didn't interrupt. I sprinted to my front door and immediately picked up my phone. Should I call 911? Am I overreacting? I thought. I decided to call Johnny first and see if he had talked to Father DeFalco last night and get his opinion on what to do. I dialed Johnny's number knowing it would ring quite a few times because I was certain he was not awake at five o'clock in the morning. The phone rang once, and Johnny picked up.

"Bags are you okay?" he said. I was breathing heavy because of sprinting from my driveway.

"Johnny, I went to Father DeFalco's this morning because we were supposed to go fishing and he never came to the door. His stuff wasn't ready, and I rang the doorbell multiple times and he never came to the door. Do you think I should call 911? I am really worried about him, Johnny," I blurted out.

"Bags, first of all, settle down. I know you are upset. I am at St. Elizabeth's hospital with Father DeFalco. I didn't know you guys were fishing this morning or I would have called you last night. Father DeFalco had a heart attack last night and was rushed here to St. Elizabeth's, and I have been waiting here with some of the other people from the church. Apparently, the Father had me listed as the first to call in an emergency," Johnny said. I was silent. I couldn't believe it. I didn't know how to react. "Bags are you okay?"

"Yes, Johnny, can I come there? How is he? What can I do?" I asked.

"Sure, just get here and we can talk," he said.

I hung up the phone, and I was literally shaking. I didn't think twice and ran out the front door to get in the car and headed straight to the hospital. I forgot to ask Johnny where he was, so I assumed he was still in the emergency room. I parked the car. My adrenaline was still flowing so my pace was rapid, and my walk was on the edge of being a run. I walked in the emergency room doors and did not see Johnny in the waiting room. I asked the nurse at the counter if Father DeFalco was there and she said he had come in late last night and has been transported to the cardiac unit on floor four. She gave me the room number and I headed straight up.

I found Johnny and some of the other clergy from the church there. Everyone was in a really gloomy mode and three clergy members had some chairs pulled close together, holding hands and praying. I could tell from the time I stepped into the waiting room that things were bad.

"How bad is it, Johnny?" I asked, a little out of breath.

"Well Bags, he is not in good shape, but the Father is a strong man and he can pull through this if it is God's will," Johnny said. There was that God's will thing again. I didn't understand why God would want Father DeFalco to die. It didn't make sense to me. Why would that ever be His will?

I asked Johnny if anyone had seen Father DeFalco, and if he was awake and responsive. He let me know that everyone had spent some time with him, and he was really weak, but he was awake and could communicate a little. I asked Johnny if he thought I could see him, and Johnny went to ask the nurse. The three clergy members were still praying intently. I paced nervously, wondering if I was going to get a chance to see the man who single-handedly changed my perspective. Johnny came back a few moments later.

"The nurse says you can go in there, but be aware he is very tired," he told me. I stood in the doorway, watching to see if he was moving. As I expected, he was hooked up to lots of monitors, and he wasn't moving at all. I stood there, wondering whether I should approach him, and then I saw him slowly open his eyes. I hated to see my mentor in such a weak, frail state. He watched me walk around the side of the bed and he smiled, or at least his facial expression changed a little as if he was trying to smile.

"This is a heck of a way to avoid going fishing with me," I said, speaking softly.

Uncomfortable as he was, he still replied. "Oh, Bags, if I didn't want to fish with you, I would have just told you to stay home. I have your bowl for you, and thanks for the soup," he said. Even in such a position he was still thanking me.

"Well how are you, you old priest?" I asked.

He responded in a soft voice that sounded like it hurt him to talk.

"I have been better, Bags, but I am one step closer to meeting my Daddy," he said. He tried to chuckle but winced in pain instead.

"Father, I hate to see you like this, but I know you are strong enough to make it through," I said.

"Well, I will if it is His will and if not, I am going home. Either way, do me a favor Bags. You are a good man. A really good man. Be confident and share yourself with someone, everyone.

The world is better with you Joey. Let me rest and go make sure Johnny isn't yelling at the clergy."

I leaned over and kissed him on the forehead and said, "Goodbye, Father DeFalco."

CHAPTER SEVENTEEN

SHARE YOU

I walked out of that room very unsure about what the future would bring for the old man. It was tough for him to talk and I could tell this was going to be quite the challenge. I approached Johnny who was in the waiting room sitting on one of the blue vinyl chairs, bent over with his head in his hands. The three clergy members were still sitting in a circle praying. I was taken aback by their ability to completely ignore their surroundings. It seemed as if they were in their own little world. I wondered if their minds wandered to overhear our conversations or not. I walked up to Johnny and touched him on the shoulder and he slowly lifted his head from his hands.

"Oh, hey Bags, how is he doing?" he asked in a very somber voice. I had never seen Johnny like this. Actually, his emotions usually extend the other way. Usually when he is upset about something, he doesn't become somber, he becomes angry and quite the handful, so I knew this was a challenging situation for him.

"Well, he is tired, but he was talking to me, and even cracked a few jokes. I think he can get through this," I said.

"Bags I'm glad to hear you say that. I'm so concerned. He is a great man and I would hate to live life without him," Johnny said.

"I know how you feel Johnny, but let's be positive," I said.

Johnny and I continued to talk for a few more minutes and then a doctor walked up to Johnny and asked to speak with him. The two of them walked away to talk, and I could tell by their body language that this was probably a tough conversation.

Then I found myself in the same blue vinyl chair that Johnny had been in, and in the same exact position with my head in my hands. Johnny tapped my shoulder lightly and I looked up to see Johnny in tears. I had never seen this before, and it caught me off guard.

"Johnny, what's wrong?" I exclaimed.

"Well, Bags it seems the old man has a serious blockage in his main heart valve, and it doesn't look good. They want to do surgery but are afraid that he may not make it at his age. They also said if he doesn't have the surgery, the chances of him having another one is very likely, and the chance of surviving the next one is slim," Johnny said.

This is not the news I wanted to hear of course, but I had to ask. "What does Father DeFalco want to do?"

Johnny was quiet for a long time. "He is not sure yet. He asked the doctor to let him pray about it overnight and he would tell them in the morning," he finally said.

It sounded like Father DeFalco was unsure if he wanted to go through the surgery. This was very concerning to me because in the time that I had known Father DeFalco, he had always been quick to make a decision and was always confident in the decisions he made. Of course, I couldn't understand why he wouldn't want to try and have the surgery. If there was a great chance of not making it, wouldn't he want to at least make an attempt? I hoped he would make the right decision, and no matter what happened, I would make sure I enjoyed the rest of my time with Father DeFalco.

I found myself pacing back and forth as if it would help me think through the situation. No matter how many times I walked back and forth, it didn't seem to make a difference. Father DeFalco was resting and was in no condition to carry on a conversation and I just couldn't sit around the hospital, so I asked Johnny if he needed anything or if he was hungry. He said he was good, and that he didn't feel much like eating anything. I looked at my watch. It was about seven thirty in the morning and I couldn't help but think that if this wasn't happening, the old man would already have three more fish in the boat than I did. I could imagine his smooth reaction, and how he guided the fish into the boat with ease. I couldn't believe that same man was now struggling to talk, struggling to breathe and couldn't even sit up. I wondered if his sickness in the last two weeks had something to do with it. Maybe he was weak from the head cold and it had put more stress on his heart. I am not sure why I was thinking that way, because, in the end, it didn't really matter. I paced for about fifteen minutes more and told Johnny that I was going to run home and get cleaned up and come back. I told him to call me if anything happened.

I drove home slower than normal, but it was not purposeful. I did recognize the fact that I was underutilizing the accelerator pedal about halfway home when a man in a black Nissan Sentra decided to blow his horn as he passed me in a no-passing zone. I was so in my own head that I wasn't even aware. When I got back to my house, Megan was backing out of the driveway, late for work. She backed up next to me and rolled down her window.

"I thought you were going fishing Joey," she yelled to me. I opened my door, stepped out, and leaned into her window.

"I got to Father DeFalco's house this morning and he wasn't there. I called Johnny and he was at the hospital with the old man. He had a heart attack and he is not doing good. I went there and spoke with him and he is very weak. I came home to get cleaned up, and then I'm going back to the hospital," I told her.

"Oh no, Bags, I am so sorry! Is there anything I can do? I know you and he had a special relationship and I know you must be concerned," said Megan. "I am late for work, honey, but I will come over as soon as I get home at seven o'clock, is that okay?"

I told her that would be fine, and she started to back down the driveway. Before she got to the end, she stopped the car.

"I love you Bags!" she yelled to me. That was the first time she had said those words.

I went into the house so that I could jump in the shower and change out of the fishing garb I had on. I walked in to find the lunch I packed for the fishing trip sitting on the counter. If I would have been giving Father DeFalco crap about not being prepared and then realized I forgot my lunch, he would have eaten that up. Oh, I could see his face now, and the whirlwind of sarcastic remarks that would start flying. Of course, they would have all been well deserved. I put the packed lunch into my refrigerator so that it didn't spoil and went to jump in the shower. I turned the shower on and went back into my room to get clean undergarments and fell down on my bed face first.

An intense moment of sadness suddenly came over me and I began to feel unbelievably lost. I started to cry, and within minutes, I was lying face down on a bedspread saturated in salty tears. It was somewhat uncontrollable, and I just kept thinking about not having father DeFalco in my life and I was feeling incredibly lonely. I knew that I had Megan and the boys in my life, but if it wasn't for the old man coaching me in that relationship, I was sure I would have screwed it up. Who was going to coach me now? My life had just begun to turn the corner for the better, and I was not confident I could do it without him. I laid on the bed and listened to the water run. I got more and more uncomfortable laying in my own tears until I finally got motivated to jump in the shower.

As I walked into the bathroom, I looked in the mirror to see the broken man that existed in the past. Not broken from my own demise but broken from despair and grief over the situation. No matter the reason, I looked broken, and that is not something I wanted to be again. I took what felt like the longest shower I have ever taken. At one point, I heard the phone ring and the answering machine beep, but I couldn't hear if anyone left a message. I usually got a call around this time multiple times a week. It came from an automated dialer, and I would hear part of a sales recording, but not enough to know what they were selling, so I assumed it was that call.

I finally got out of the shower and I started to feel refreshed. I remembered what Father DeFalco said to me about sharing myself and realized that no one would want to share me like this. I had to pull myself out of the funk and get myself together.

I decided to throw on some good clothes. That always made me feel better because it makes me look important. I had a great pair of navy blue, never-iron dress pants and a white button up dress shirt that made me feel polished. If I was going back to the hospital, I wanted to feel good about myself to offset the emotions of despair the situation was bringing. Then I put on my brown dress shoes which I probably hadn't worn in the last two years. I had to dust them off from the bottom of the closet. Before I left, I made a pitcher of iced tea and poured some into a large to-go cup that I got as a souvenir from a Cleveland Browns football game and headed for the door to get back to the hospital.

I took a step out the front door and remembered that I had heard the answering machine and never checked it. I stepped back into the house and the screen door slammed shut. I kept meaning to change out the cylinder that is supposed to stop it from slamming, but I kept forgetting to get one. I set my cup of tea on the kitchen counter and hit play. There was a message I somehow missed from Megan the night before wishing me a good night. She had a soft voice that was so pleasant to hear so I hit the save button because I wanted to listen to it again. The next message was the one left while I was in the shower and it was from Johnny.

"Joey it's Johnny. Please call me back as soon as you get this."

I got a nervous feeling in my stomach, partly because of

the tone of his voice, and partly because he called me Joey. I can't remember the last time Johnny called me Joey. In fact, I am not sure he ever has. I quickly grabbed the phone and dialed Johnny's number.

Johnny answered the phone on the second ring

"Hold on a minute Bags," he said. I could hear him talking to someone.

"Are you still there?" he said finally. "I wanted to call you and tell you that you don't have to come back to the hospital. Bags, Father DeFalco didn't make it. He has gone to meet his Father and I am certain they are happy to see each other."

I sat silently on the phone for quite some time until Johnny asked if I was still there.

"Yes. What's next Johnny? How can I help?" I asked.

"There isn't much to be done. The coroner will get his body in a few hours and we will wait to hear from the church in regard to when the services will be. I contacted Father DeFalco's brother who lives in New Mexico, and he was going to jump on the earliest flight here. For right now, Bags, we just wait until we hear more. I am sure the church will put together a wonderful service, and I am sure he would want you there."

"I will be there Johnny. Do you mind if I take some time off? I have to work through this. This is a tough one for me, Johnny," I said. Again, there was a long moment of silence. Then I heard Johnny sniffle.

"Take as much time as you need, Joey. I understand."

I hung up the phone and looked down at my brown dress

shoes to see stains from my tear drops. I couldn't believe he was gone. I took off my dress clothes and crawled in bed. I didn't want to see anyone or talk to anyone. I was lying in bed thinking about all of the wisdom the Father had shared with me over the seven or eight months I knew him. I got up out of bed and grabbed my notebook and reviewed the pages. I remembered the last thing the Father said to me and grabbed a pen to add the last bit of wisdom I would ever receive from him. I remembered the words exactly, and I never wanted to forget them. I wrote, "Be confident and share yourself with someone, everyone. The world is better with you." His final words of encouragement for me. I will never forget them.

Then I took some over-the-counter sleeping medication and fell asleep. Later in the afternoon, I heard a knock on my door, and I was certain it was Megan. Then I heard my phone ring a few times and I didn't answer. I really didn't want to talk to anyone. I was lying there feeling guilty for not communicating with Megan. I knew she cared, so I called her and let her know of Father DeFalco's passing and told her that I just needed some time to myself this evening. She understood and was amazingly compassionate and supportive. She asked if I needed anything.

"Some alone time is all I need," I told her. She obliged and gave me the space I needed. I went back to bed and tried to sleep this whole day off.

CHAPTER EIGHTEEN

THE MOURNING AFTER

The next morning, I woke early because I had slept the whole day prior. I was still in a mood of total despair. It didn't really make sense because the last conversation I had with the old man was a good one. He seemed as if he was at peace, and somewhat excited to get to heaven. I started to think that I was incapable of thinking that way, and I couldn't be joyous now that he was gone. Maybe it was because I am selfish or maybe because I simply couldn't imagine another existence beyond this physical world. Truthfully, it was probably a little of both. I was never good at visualizing anything beyond what I could physically touch, unless, of course, you consider my ability to visualize the worst-case scenario. I am really good at making those up in my mind, and they often come true. However, I had not visualized what happened to Father DeFalco. It may be the worst thing that had ever happened to me. At least at that moment, it felt that way.

I dragged myself to the kitchen to boost my step with a little artificial stimulant. I grabbed the bag of coffee and filled the pot with water, only to find out I was out of coffee filters. I stopped and leaned against the kitchen counter. This is going to be one of those days. Then I remembered that this happened to me in the past, and I used a paper towel instead. It was certainly not the best solution, but it would allow me to get some coffee down the hatch. So, I tore off a paper towel and formed it into the section where the coffee filter is supposed to go. I put it back together and hit the brew button and went to the bathroom to freshen up a little bit. Again, I looked in the mirror and did not like what I saw. I ran some cold water in the sink and grabbed a clean washcloth to wipe my face with cold water. It did feel refreshing, and it did make me feel a little more alive. I wasn't going to shake this feeling easily, but maybe I could see some light.

Just then the phone rang, and it was Johnny.

"Bags, I wanted to call you and let you know the funeral is scheduled for Wednesday afternoon at three o'clock. You know how many people the old man influenced, so I am sure it will be packed. So, get there early. Oh yeah, take your time getting back to work. I was able to get your shifts covered."

"Thanks Johnny, I appreciate that, and I will get there early," I said. I couldn't believe I was saying I would be early to a place I was so sad to go. I did, however, think about Father DeFalco and how he would want me to be prepared. There was nothing I could do to prepare for this. I knew it was going to be one of the most challenging events of my life. Johnny and I quickly hung up the phone, since I assumed that he had many people to call, and I was just one on his list of many. I turned to see if my coffee was done brewing, when I heard a knock on the door. I would recognize that knock every time.

I opened the door to see Megan standing there dressed like a little tomboy with a baseball hat and old cut-up jeans. Oddly enough, I still found this very attractive on Megan. She had a sad look on her face which I chalked up to her look of compassion and empathy for the loss of a good friend and someone that had a major impact on our relationship, whether she recognized that or not. I opened the door and Megan stepped inside and wrapped her arms around my mid-section tighter than I had ever been held before, but somehow it still felt so warm and soft.

"Bags I am so sorry. I know how much you loved Father DeFalco," she said softly. She wasn't wrong there.

"I did love him, Megan, and I don't know what I am going to do without him. Johnny called me this morning and told me the funeral is at three o'clock on Wednesday. Can you go with me? I am not sure if you want the boys to go or not," I said.

"I will absolutely go with you, Bags, and I will find someone to watch the boys. I am not sure they should see that at their age," she said. I understood this. I was nine when I went to my first funeral and I would never forget it. It gave me nightmares and I didn't deal with it well. Even at my age, I am going to have to work up to this one.

Megan and I sat together and reminisced about our times with the old man for the next hour or so. I shared stories with her about Father DeFalco peeing off the front of the boat and a wave causing him to soak the whole front of his pants. I shared how much I admired how he taught me, how patient he was with me and the unreal amount of wisdom he shared with me until the day he died. I did not share what he told me the day he died because I thought there would be a better time and place to do that. Talking with Megan made me feel better and I was happy she came over. She then asked if we could go to lunch, and I was feeling a little hungry, so I agreed to join her. I went to the bathroom to brush my teeth. When I came out of the bathroom,

Megan wiped the toothpaste out of the corner of my mouth, and we laughed.

"Don't worry, Joey, I'll make sure you put your pants on before you head out in public," she said. I believe she was making reference to the fact that I looked like a mess. I always liked the fact that she felt comfortable enough with me to give me jabs like that. We walked out to get in the car without even knowing where we were going.

Megan insisted she drive and said she knew of a great little place that she wanted to take me, if I was up for some pizza. She was starting to know me pretty well. Nothing cheers me up more than a good pizza. We started driving and I was not sure she realized she was going to drive right by Father DeFalco's house. She couldn't know because she had never been there. As we drove by, I got a huge ball of discomfort in my gut. His truck was still sitting in the same spot as it was when I went to pick him up that morning. Now come to think of it, I had left my four rods in the rod holder, but it didn't matter much because I had no one to fish with. As we went by, I pointed out his house to Megan. I told her what a great little place it was and made reference to the truck and boat being just like it was the other day.

"Bags, I'm sorry for driving you past there. I was attempting to cheer you up not kick you when you're down," she said.

"I know that," I told her, "and you didn't know where he lived so I know it couldn't have been on purpose."

She took me to this little wood-fired pizza place that

was amazing. The dough was tossed in front of you and they had some really great specialty pizzas. I got one called the Bruschetta which included pesto sauce, fresh tomatoes, fresh basil leaves, fresh mozzarella cheese and it was drizzled on top with this thick balsamic sauce. It was awesome. She got a vegetarian pizza, which normally I would scoff at, but the pizza was really good. We enjoyed each other's company and for a moment, I forgot about what happened, and counted my blessings. After all, that was exactly what the old man would tell me to do if he still could. He would tell me to recognize all of the good I had and forget about the bad. I was feeling much better.

"I am glad to see you smiling again, Bags," Megan said as we finished eating our pizza. "There are lots of people around you that love you and will help you through this."

"Thank you, Megan," I said.

We drove back home and when we went by Father DeFalco's house, there was a car in the driveway. I was not sure who it was, and I didn't see anyone outside. I guess it could have been family, although he never talked about his family much. I am sure there would be lots of people in and out as they settled the estate. I thought I should just try to forget about it until Wednesday and enjoy my time with Megan and the boys. So, that is exactly what I did.

Unfortunately, they were gone most of the day, so I found myself doing useless stuff around my house. On Monday and Tuesday I cooked dinner for them and had it ready when they got home from school and work. It felt like a family. We sat at the table together, and both days it felt odd without Father DeFalco there to say the blessing. In fact, young Joey mentioned that he felt we should say a blessing. He only said it after we all had our faces stuffed and no one felt like we could go backwards.

"You're right, Joey, maybe next time you can say it," Megan suggested.

On Wednesday morning, I got up early and felt pretty good. I started my coffee and jumped in the shower. When I got out of the shower, I could hear my phone ringing. I tied the towel around my waist and ran to get the phone. I answered, and it was Johnny. He told me that the last couple days, he had been helping to go through Father DeFalco's will and settle his estate. I told him I saw a car in the driveway and assumed that is what they were doing there. He then went on to tell me that they read his will at the attorney's office and that I was mentioned. He asked if I had a minute so he could read it to me, and I said yes.

"I want to leave my boat, my truck, and all my fishing gear to my best fishing partner, Joey "Bags" Alfieri. Please ask him to put it to good use," Johnny read. I was stunned. I had only been fishing with the old man for seven or eight months. He must have written this in his will recently, almost like he knew he was dying soon.

"Wow, Johnny, that is amazing. I can't believe that," I replied.

Johnny got a little lump in his throat. "Yes, Bags, it's obvious that Father DeFalco thought very highly of you. The company hired to take care of the estate will bring them by sometime today and I can help you get the title transferred and get the tags," he said. I hung up the phone in utter disbelief.

Megan was going to work a half day and then come home so we could get ready to go. Since she was gone, I decided to go get some breakfast. I went to the local diner where Father DeFalco used to tell me he went all the time. He said he came to our restaurant for cinnamon rolls and to this little local diner called "The Greasy Spoon" for omelets and bacon. I went in and was probably the youngest person in the place by thirty years or more. They had a special called "The Father" which was a ham and cheese omelet with jalapeño peppers and five slices of bacon. I ordered that from the waitress, and she asked if I knew Father DeFalco.

"Yes, he was a good friend," I said. She asked me what my name was, and I introduced myself.

Her eyes widened. "You're Bags? Honey we have heard so much about you. Your breakfast is on us this morning. Father DeFalco loved you, young man. I am so sorry for your loss," she said.

When she walked away, I saw her telling the other waitresses and customers that I was Bags. It made me think about how much Father DeFalco cared about me. It definitely went both ways.

I finished at the diner, drove back home and saw Megan was there. I pulled in the driveway at the same time she was getting out of her car. I got out and gave her a hug. I held her so tight and pushed her back away from me a little so she could see my face.

"The most amazing thing just happened," I told her. "Father DeFalco left his boat and truck for me in his will. I also just came from the diner he used to go to, and everyone there treated me like a celebrity. The Father told everyone in there about me. I couldn't believe it. Even if he is not here, I am still getting surprised by the things he has done."

Megan looked at me with compassion in her eyes. "Well, Bags, I think he really did have a man crush on you. Now let's go and get ready to pay our final respects to this amazing man," she said.

CHAPTER NINETEEN

ONE FISH

Megan went into her house to get ready, and I went inside to find the phone was ringing. I rushed to grab it, and found it was Johnny just checking on me. He wanted to make sure I was getting ready and was going to get there early. He said he was saving a seat for me in the front with close family and friends of the Father. I told him that Megan was coming with me and asked him to make sure to save two seats if it was not a problem. I asked what time we should get there.

"Well, Bags, I am here now, and we are expecting over five hundred people to pay their respects, so I would get here as soon as you can," he said. "Then you get to pay your respects early and not have to wait in a big line."

Thanks for thinking of me," I said, "and both Megan and I will see you soon."

I hung up the phone and thought about the fact that I had really only explored a true relationship with Father DeFalco over the last year, other than the jokes in passing at the restaurant, and now I was sitting with close family and friends. I guess it was really not about the amount of time you know someone, it was really about the impact they make on your life. I wasn't sure what kind of an impact I could have made in his life, but I was certain of the impact he had made on mine. At that moment I was wondering if I could continue my progress without him. I supposed I had no choice.

It was time to get ready to pay my final respects and I was hoping the only suit I owned was in good shape. I went into the back of my closet and found the suit bag and laid it on my bed. I unzipped the bag and found the suit looking pretty good. Then I remembered that I had it dry cleaned after the last time I wore it so that it would be ready to go the next time I needed it. I chuckled to myself that Father DeFalco would have been proud of that preparation. I also had my white shirt in the back dry cleaned and ready to go.

I jumped in the shower and kept thinking about Johnny saying, "the earlier I get there the better." I thought that I should have let Megan know so she would hurry. I got in and out of the shower and threw on my t-shirt, socks, and underwear, and I ran to the phone to call Megan. She answered on the second ring. I let her know what Johnny said, and she told me she was ready now. She was awesome! Not only was she beautiful and compassionate but she was prompt and low maintenance.

I went back and finished getting ready. I wondered if I should wear a tie or not, because I never wore ties. It was something I said I was never going to do after I left my corporate job. I thought maybe I should, but then realized I didn't even have a tie. The choice was simple then. It took me about fifteen minutes to finish getting ready, and then I headed over to Megan's so we could get going. The closer it came to the funeral, the more uneasy I was becoming.

I rang Megan's doorbell and she promptly opened the door and invited me in as she finished putting tissues in her handbag. I assumed she was thinking she was going to need those at some point during the service. She was wearing the same black dress she had on when she first met Father DeFalco at my house. Her hair was down, and she looked stunning. I made mention that she was wearing the dress she had on when she first met Father DeFalco.

"I know Bags, I thought it would be appropriate and I remembered I had this on the night we all had dinner together. What a great night," she said. I agreed, and we headed to the car to get this day underway.

As we walked to the car, I glanced over at Megan and couldn't believe I was lucky enough to have a girl like her interested in me. I also thought that if it weren't for the man, we were about to pay respects to, I would have surely screwed it up by now. Thanks to him I am getting in my car with the most beautiful woman I have ever seen, and on top of that, she liked me.

The ride to the church was not full of lively conversation like it was most often when Megan and I were together. We spoke, but it was very matter of fact and to the point. Mostly discussing the logistics of the day. I understood from Johnny that there was not going to be a service at the cemetery because Father DeFalco requested not to have one. The Father said he had performed so many services at the cemetery and just wasn't a fan of it. The Father requested to celebrate the raising of his spirit and not mourn in the burial of his flesh. That sounded like something the Father would say and I know he believed wholeheartedly that his spirit was in Heaven with the Lord. So today would be services at the church, and no one was going to witness the Father be put in the ground. I thought this was probably a good thing because it was going to be hard enough to witness the old man in the casket. Megan didn't know it but before I went to the diner, I went over to Father DeFalco's house and cut off that white and pink deep diver crankbait that he caught so many fish on. I thought if there were places in Heaven to go fishing, he would want his number one bait.

We pulled in the church parking lot about an hour and a half early. My palms were beginning to sweat, and I asked Megan if we could just sit in the car for a few minutes. She obliged and she sat, seemingly uncomfortable as well. We watched a few of the clergy members walk into the church. The parking lot only had ten or so cars in it, so I knew we made it early enough to beat the crowd.

I laid my head on the steering wheel, just thinking about the times we had together on the water. There was something about the relationship you have with a fishing partner. You have the same common passion, trying to achieve what no one else has and doing it in a way where you support each other and celebrate the victories together. You prepare together, count on the strategy you come up with, plan the day, and work together to execute the plan. It is a true partnership, and maybe that's the reason you say, "fishing partner" not "fishing friend" or "fishing companion." It is a fishing partner, someone who has your back, who works together with you to achieve a goal and who finds joy when you succeed. I lifted my head from the steering wheel.

"I think I am ready to go see my fishing partner," I said to Megan.

By this time about three more cars were in the parking lot, and another two were pulling in as we stepped out of the car. I grabbed my suit jacket from the backseat where I put it so it wouldn't wrinkle and put it on. I shut my car door and I waited for Megan to come around the front of the car. I put my arm out so we could lock arms. I thought the two of us made a great looking couple. It was too bad the Father couldn't see us now. He would be proud.

Suddenly, I had the feeling that he did see us, and he was proud. We walked in the door of the church and as expected, it was quite a depressing atmosphere: The music, the lighting, the way the workers greeted you with their hands folded in front of them and saying how sorry they are for your loss. Megan and I walked up to the register on the pedestal and signed our names as guests. We were the fifth and sixth people who had signed it and once again, I thought how the Father would approve of our promptness.

We turned the corner into the room with the casket, and it was beautiful. I have never in my life seen so many flowers in one room. It was mind-blowing, and the fragrance of fresh flowers that filled the room was incredible. It felt like every two to three steps would give you a different aroma.

Johnny was standing in the front, speaking to an older couple I did not know, and Megan and I kind of stood awkwardly towards the back of the room. I could see Father DeFalco's face from a distance, and it created a higher sense of nervousness. We stood there for a few minutes until Megan finally spoke.

"Let's go see our friend, Bags. I know it's tough but let's get it over with so we can remember the good times," she said. I hesitantly agreed and we slowly walked toward the casket. As we approached, I recognized he had on what he fondly referred to as his monkey suit. He looked very nice and at first, I found myself evaluating whether he looked realistic or not. I noticed a small blue spot on the back of his hand that was probably where the IV was when he was in the hospital, and the makeup just couldn't completely cover the bruise.

I was holding Megan's hand, and that helped my comfort level, but when I looked deeply at the Father's face, the realization of the finality set in. I tried to hold back the emotion and I was unsuccessful. My face began to feel pressurized like when you shake a can of soda. Then the pressure was released with an overwhelming amount of emotions and tears. Megan and I released hands and now and she was solely focused on comforting me by rubbing my back. She was quiet and comforted me with her touch and not her words. She knew it was all she could do.

I began to get control of myself and tried to consciously question why this hurt so bad. I mustered up enough strength to remember the fishing lure I brought with me. His hands were folded together neatly on top of his waist. I decided to take the lure and put it near his hands so he could grab it when he needed to tie up. I looked at his body and remembered him reaching for his rod and muscling those big old fish to the boat just a short time ago. The realization of how fast it ends was setting into my mind and I started to feel the pressure in my face again and asked Megan if we could walk away now.

"Absolutely, babe."

I had never heard her me call babe before, and I think it was another way to show her compassion. We walked towards the back of the room and the further we moved away from the casket, the more my tears dried. Johnny came back and hugged me and kissed me on the cheek and did the same to Megan. He told us where he had saved us seats.

For the next hour we greeted lots of people. We live in a fairly small town, so both Megan and I knew quite a few people, and we found ourselves introducing each other. At first it was a little awkward because we didn't know if we should introduce each other as friend or girlfriend and boyfriend, so after about the second introduction she introduced me as Joey, and I introduced her as Megan. All of the talking made time go fast and it seemed like in no time at all we were asked to take our seats.

I noticed the old couple that I saw talking to Johnny was now sitting next to him. I assumed that it was Father DeFalco's brother that Johnny had mentioned was coming in from out of town. The more I looked at him, the more I saw the old man in him. He was obviously younger but had similar features. The funeral service began and was similar to other Catholic funerals I have attended. There was the procession of the priest, and he sprinkled the coffin with holy water, and Johnny was asked to read a passage from the Bible. I wasn't sure it was from the old or new testament; I am not that familiar. There was a young priest who was giving the message, and he started by saying what a mentor Father DeFalco had been to him, and I could totally relate. He then went on to talk about all of the amazing wisdom he obtained from Father DeFalco, and I could relate again. The next part set me back on my heels. I couldn't believe it.

The young priest was visibly moved by what he was about to say. "Some of you know that Father DeFalco had some very interesting ways about him. I am going to share with you all one of those interesting things that only a few us knew. Over the last two years Father DeFalco was very vocal that he was ready and prepared to go home and be with his Father. It wasn't that he had given up on life or was any less passionate about his role here on Earth. It was merely his way of saying, I have confessed my sins, I have repented, and I know where I am going next. Whenever the good Lord says it is my time, I am ready. Because of this he made it his mission to have a current message ready for you whenever it was his time. So, every week he wrote a message that was to be shared with all of you if God took him sometime during that week. He put it in a safe every week and told a few of us where the combination was. So, here is the last message from Father DeFalco to all of you."

Wow! I was about to hear the final words of wisdom from the old man. I only wish I had brought my notebook with me.

The young priest opened up a sealed envelope and began to read. "Dear members of our congregation, I want to start by saying thank you for allowing me to have the honor of leading our church. It is humbling to be in a position where you are felt loved by so many people and I wish all of you the best. I hope that God used me to inspire you with His word. I want you all to acknowledge that if you believe I have made any impact on your life, you are wrong. I was simply delivering the message. The message was not mine; it was my Father's who I am with in Heaven today. To all of my clergy: stay focused on the hearts of our people and not so much to the rigors of the church. God is love, and we are called to love one another like He loves us...unconditionally. To those of you in the room who are not believers, please take the time explore the Bible and let God speak to you through it. It will change your life. Lastly, to my fishing partner Bags. I am sorry for missing the last couple weeks with a head cold. I wanted so badly to be on the water with you. I am proud of who you are becoming and proud to call you the best fishing partner I ever had. I will have our rods and everything prepared for you when you get to Heaven. Please find your way here. Until then, invest in others, share yourself with that cute little girl next door and be patient because you must remember: One Fish Changes Everything. John 3:16.

At that point the pressure was once again building in my face, and tears were starting to flow. I don't remember the rest of the service, but the old man had made his final impact, and it was a big one.

CHAPTER TWENTY

TIGHT LINES

After the service, we said goodbye to everyone and as Megan and I walked across the parking lot she asked if I was okay.

"I know that was tough for you, Bags, but you have to feel really good about the impact you made on Father DeFalco. He actually wrote you a message to tell you how much he believes in you. I thought that was incredible," she said.

I agreed with Megan but somehow, I still felt like I was lost. She could tell I was twisted up with emotion, and she continued to try to counsel me the whole way home. The drive was slow, and I was reflecting on the times we had together and the wisdom he filled me with each and every trip.

I thought about the message he wrote for me and I was going to go home and write the words he said in great big capital letters. One fish changes everything. If I recall, he said that to me before, and I think it is already in my book, but it seemed more impactful to me today. I also thought about how he ended the message with John 3:16. I remember looking that up one time because I saw a guy at the super bowl holding a great big sign in the end zone that had that written on it. Honestly, I can't remember what it said.

When we pulled onto my street, I asked Megan if she had a Bible.

"Yes, I have on old one, but I will have to find it. Can I bring it over to you later?" she said.

"Yes, that will be fine, no hurry," I replied. As we got closer to the house, I saw that someone had left Father DeFalco's truck and boat in my driveway. I told Megan that I was sorry that it is sitting there, and I was going to have to find a place to keep it.

"Are you kidding me, Bags, it's fine right where it is. You should be excited," I told her I was excited, but it just isn't going to be the same fishing without the old man next to me. I told her I just couldn't imagine getting out on the boat alone. "I know, Bags, but Father DeFalco wanted you to have that boat and he would be disappointed if you didn't get out on the water with it," she said. I agreed with her and told her she was right, but I would have to wait and see when I could get out there.

Megan went to go pick up the boys from the babysitter and I told her I was going to go inside and take a nap. I told her to just ring the doorbell if she found her Bible when she got back. She said she would. I hugged her once again and we went our separate ways into our homes.

When I went in, I went straight to the bedroom to get out of my suit and put some sweatpants on. As soon as I got changed, the doorbell rang, and Megan was at the door with her Bible.

"Hey Bags, turns out I knew where it was after all. I decided to bring it over before I went to get the boys," she said. I told her thanks and I would see her later. I took the Bible from her and went back into my bedroom and laid down on my bed.

I flipped through the Bible, looking for John, and it took me a while, but I finally found it and turned to John 3:16 and read it. It said, *For God so loved the world, that he gave his one and only Son, that whoever believes in him shall not perish, but have eternal life.* I pondered that for a while and realized that Father DeFalco wanted me to believe in Jesus. He had talked to me about that before, and I just wasn't there yet. I continued to read, and I remembered Father DeFalco telling me what I read in John 3:27: A person can receive only what is given him from heaven. The old man truly believed in a higher power, and no matter how well you did everything else, success was contingent upon that. That is why he always said, "if it is His will." He was always prepared, built great plans, but would always seem to know it was never completely under his control.

I closed the Bible and turned sideways on my pillow to take a nap. I fell asleep quickly and woke up to the doorbell ringing again. I looked out the door and saw Megan and the boys. I opened the door.

"Excuse me," Megan said, "is this where Father DeFalco's favorite fishing partner lives? Are you him? If so, I would like to cash in my certificate, and Joey said he would like to join you on the boat tomorrow. I spoke to his teachers and told them he is going to miss a day from school, and I will make sure he gets caught up on his homework." I just woke up and was a little confused but then I recognized the certificate I had given Megan months earlier for a day babysitting one of her boys.

"Well Joey, do you think you can handle being on the boat with me? Do you think we can catch some fish?" I asked. Joey nodded his head in a rapid fashion and his eyes were lit up like a thousand stars.

"Well, I am not sure I have enough time to get everything prepared unless I have someone to help me," I said.

"I can help! I can help!" Joey quickly responded.

"Well then, Joey, give me a few minutes and we will get the boat organized and ready to go." Megan leaned towards me, planted a kiss on my lips and grabbed both sides of my face in her hands.

"I love you Joey Alfieri. I hope you guys catch a bunch," she said.

Joey and I worked to get everything ready in the boat. There wasn't a whole lot to do but it gave me time to walk Joey through what we would do when we got onto the water in the morning. I also showed him the electronics and how to work the trolling motor. We would use the same strategy I put together for the trip the Father and I were going to take on Saturday. We were going to anchor and jig minnow or nightcrawler-tipped jigs near another roadbed that Father DeFalco showed me one day.

I helped Joey tie his jigs on his lines and let him pick what color he wanted to use. He wanted a black one at first and explained that black wasn't good with the current water color. I explained that black is typically used with muddy water, and he then decided to change it to chartreuse. It was fun to teach him those things, and like when we were cleaning fish, he was absorbing it all. I hoped Joey would be okay on the boat, but the way he had been helping and learning, I am sure he would be fine. I looked forward to spending the day with him, and I was going to make sure I did just what Father DeFalco told me. He said to invest in others. In fact, I was going to read through my notebook tonight to make sure I was heeding the old man's wishes.

Joey and I finished up and I told Joey to be at my house at five thirty in the morning and not to be late. I told him I would pack him a lunch and asked him if he liked chocolate soda. He had never had it, but I was sure he would like it, so I packed him a couple cans.

That evening I was lying in bed reading through my notebook of wisdom from Father DeFalco, and I made sure to write down his message from the funeral. *Always remember, one fish changes everything.* Helping young Joey catch a few nice ones would be great. I couldn't believe I was going on the Father's boat without him, but I would be thinking about him the entire time.

I noticed that I still had Megan's Bible in my room, and I opened it and started reading. I didn't get very far before I became sleepy. Maybe I would try again some other time but right then, I needed to get some sleep to be ready when young Joey showed up in the morning.

My alarm woke me at five o'clock and I was moving a little slowly. I had programmed my coffee to start brewing at 4:45 a.m. and I could smell the aroma in the air. I put on my pants and went to the kitchen to get a cup. I could see through my front door that the light was on at Megan's.

I opened my door and saw Joey all bundled up and sitting on the rocking chair on the front porch. I yelled for him to come over. I gave him his lunch and told him to go throw it in the cooler in the boat. I looked out and saw Megan coaching him from the porch in her robe with her arms crossed tightly to help drive some warmth to her mid-section. I finished my coffee, grabbed the rest of my stuff and walked over to say goodbye to Megan. She never unlocked her arms but kissed me on the cheek, said to be careful, and told both Joey and I that she hoped we caught the biggest fish in the lake.

"I am not worried about that, but I sure hope I can get Joey to catch a few," I told her quietly.

Joey and I pulled out of the driveway and it felt really odd driving the old man's truck. In fact, I started to think about how I have taken the driver's seat and looked over at the little man next to me, and realized I am driving far more than this truck or boat. This was my opportunity to influence Joey like Father used to influence me. We pulled into the bait shop to get minnows and Joey went in with me. Captain Mark was working behind the counter.

"Hey Bags, who is your little friend? And I am so sorry to hear about Father DeFalco. I hope you know how much you meant to him," Captain Mark said. I smiled at him.

"This is my neighbor, Joey, and yes, I sure have found out the last few days. He left his boat and truck to me. It's crazy. Nothing will ever beat fishing with the old man, but young Joey and I are gonna give it our best," I said. Captain Mark wished us both luck and we ran back out to the boat and set the minnow bucket in the live well and made sure it was secured.

We pulled into the state park boat ramp, and it was really quiet. There was a single loon out on the lake that would wail from time to time, but there was no one around, and I couldn't see another boat on the lake. I guess it was because it was a weekday. I was thinking it would take a little while getting the boat in the water by myself, so it was probably a good thing there was no one waiting.

I backed the boat down the ramp and told Joey he could get on the boat. I stopped the boat before it hit the water and showed Joey how to walk down from the trailer and climb into the front of the boat. "Awesome!" he exclaimed, like he had been doing with everything I had taught him. I showed him how to throw the rope to me on the dock when I backed him off the trailer. I slowly backed down until the boat loosened up but didn't quite come completely off the trailer. I got out of the truck, walked out on the dock, and told Joey to throw me the rope. He threw it perfectly and hit me right in the hands. I used the rope to pull the boat off the trailer, tied it to the dock, and told Joey to wait here until I parked the truck.

I quickly parked the truck and ran back down to the boat. I was chuckling to myself because we did that in half the time it would take the Father and me. The old man's shuffle wasn't the fastest part of the trip. I climbed in the boat, primed the fuel line, turned the key, and it fired right up. The sun was just starting to come up, and there was just enough light for us to navigate across the lake. I told Joey to bundle up and hold on.

We zoomed across the lake. Joey's teeth were probably freezing because he hadn't stopped smiling the whole ride across the water. As we pulled into the creek arm, there was a good amount of fog hanging right on top of the water. I was sure it would burn off quickly as the sun kept rising. I had told Joey the night before about needing his help with the anchor. I turned on the electronics and I could see the roadbed. I wanted to put us right on top of it because we had gotten out there early enough that they may still be chasing bait and feeding.

I asked Joey if he remembered how I had showed him to drop the anchor. "Yes Mr. Bags."

I told him to get up front and drop it on my command. Then I pulled forward about twenty feet and told him to drop it. I told him to tell me when it hits the bottom and he did. Then I put the boat in reverse and told him to keep letting the line out. I yelled to secure the line and he remembered exactly how to tie it like I showed him in the driveway last night. I threw the other anchor off the back of the boat, let it hit the bottom, and pulled it tight. It was time to fish.

I told Joey to get a minnow out of the bucket and showed him how to hook it on his jig. The day before, we had practiced in my driveway how to move the fishing rod. He had been so spot on, I didn't feel the need to remind him how to do it. The fog was still lingering right on top the water I told him to drop his line in and let it go to the bottom and I did exactly the same.

In a moment of silence, I had a really strange feeling come over me. I wasn't sure if it was guilt because I was already enjoying myself without the old man there. It was a really odd feeling and I couldn't shake it. I started to think through all the steps the Father and I would do to make sure I wasn't forgetting something. I went step by step and the only thing I didn't do was pray.

As strange as it felt, I bowed my head and closed my eyes. "God, if there is a God, thank you for giving Joey and I the opportunity to be here today. Thank you for allowing me to get to know Father DeFalco and if he is by you right now, tell him I love him and thank him for everything. Please keep us safe, and if it is your will, please let us catch some fish today. Amen."

I opened my eyes and looked up and saw little Joey with his head bowed. I smiled because it was great to have him on board. Just then, Joey's rod went blasting toward the water. It was still in his hands, and his head rose up in a flash. His eyes were wide open and both hands were clenched on his rod. I put my rod in the rod holder, facing the rear of the boat, and I coached him through keeping his rod tip up and getting a reel on the fish. He fought and fought and at one point, he wanted to hand me the rod and I refused. This was his fish to fight.

Finally, I saw some silver coming through the water, and I grabbed the net and coached him through guiding the fish into the net. It was a great walleye, probably about six and a half pounds. I gave Joey a high five and congratulated him. He was completely out of breath. I quickly got the fish into the live well. As soon as I had thrown it in there, I heard a noise behind me, and turned to see that my rod in the rod holder was pegged and the line was stripping off the reel.

I grabbed it, and it felt huge. My first thought is that I had hooked a flathead catfish because there was no way this could be a walleye. I fought this fish for what felt like an eternity. Little Joey's mouth never stopped the whole time, but I am not sure

I could tell you a single word he said. I was too focused on getting whatever I had on the line into the boat. I kept thinking I was going to get a glimpse of the fish and it would take off again, ripping more line off of my reel. Little Joey had the net in his hand.

"Joey, I am going to need you to help me get the fish into the net," I told him. He nodded his head nervously. "You can do it, just hold onto the handle tight and bury the net in the water, and I will drag it in," I said.

Just then, I finally got a glimpse of the fish. It was silver, far too silver to be a catfish. It was starting to slow down and wear out, and I gave a long steady pull, revealing that it was the biggest walleye I had ever seen in my life. My heart was pounding out of my chest. I couldn't believe it. I told Joey to get ready and get the net in the water. He buried it in there, and I slowly dragged the beast into the net headfirst, where it gave a final head jerk. The line came, free but it was in the net. I dropped my rod and both Joey and I grabbed the net and hauled it into the boat. It was the biggest, most beautiful fish I had ever seen.

Joey helped me muscle it up and get it onto a scale to weigh it. The scale read twelve pounds and fifteen ounces. It was a new lake record! I looked at Joey and it was like I was back at the funeral. The pressure in my face built up and tears started to fly.

"What's wrong, Mr. Bags? What's wrong?" Joey asked. I looked back at Joey and wiped my eyes.

"I'm sorry Joey, nothing's wrong. Promise me you will never forget what I am about to tell you, Joey," I said.

"I promise Mr. Bags," he said with anticipation.

I attempted to reply as the tears started to flow again. I looked up to see a real look of concern on young Joey's face. I walked to the front of the boat with my back turned to Joey, trying to get my composure. I tilted my head back and looked up at the clouds and wondered if the old man was smiling in Heaven. I finally turned back to Joey and said, "Just remember this young man. ONE FISH CHANGES EVERYTHING."

EPILOGUE

Thank you for reading *One Fish Changes Everything*. It shouldn't surprise anyone to find out that I have a real passion for fishing myself. As I grew in my professional career, I started to draw correlations between what would make me successful on the water and what would make me successful in business or in life. I also recognized through my fishing adventures that there are fishermen of all different levels. There are those who pull up a lawn chair to the edge of the water, put a worm on their line, cast it out and sit and wait to see what happens. That is what they enjoy. There are others who take it a little more serious and will walk the shoreline for hours casting into all the tricky spots. Then there are those who spend their time learning the science of fishing, the patterns of species, the effects of weather fronts, water temperature and color of the water, the impact from moon phases, the timing of spawning patterns...I can go on and on. My whole point here is that, in life, you have to decide what kind of fisherman you want to be.

I am certain these correlations can be found with lots of things, but it comes down to the fact that your chances of success in business and in life are directly proportionate to how much thought and action you put into it. Many people fail at managing their finances because they never learned the basics. They did not have a good foundation. Many people fail at achieving their financial goals because they went too wide and chased ten different things instead of defining a target and aggressively going after it. Many people fail to get to the next level of what they are doing because they put together a strategy that was short-term goal related instead of visionary with no limits. Finally, people often put together a plan that is impossible to execute. The fact is, we all fish in the same lakes and some people consistently catch them and some don't. Some catch really big fish, and some put the same time in on the same body of water and never catch one worth talking about.

What I have learned over the years is that humans generally tend to overcomplicate things. We tend to take things that are simple and make them seem so complex because we tie our emotions into them. We overthink things because we are unsure how people will respond, and we end up doing nothing. All the successful people I have met in my life have figured out that it is not that complicated. They do not get emotional. They make clear decisions based on data, and most of all, they plan, prepare, act and adjust. I also know that most really successful people fail far more than they succeed, but they keep it in perspective and never stop trying.

I hope that you enjoyed reading the story of Bags and you learned valuable lessons from both the wisdom of Father DeFalco and Bag's relationships with others. Father DeFalco broke down the mystery of catching a giant fish into simple steps. Have the right foundation, define your target, develop your strategy and build your plan. To execute the plan, you have to be prepared, diligent, and willing to adjust. It doesn't take much more than that. Keep your emotions out of it and move forward with vigor, confidence, and a fear of nothing. Wipe away the thoughts of you not having the right education or not being smart enough and do what you do best and invest in others on your journey. That will pay back over and over in your heart and your ability to succeed. God created you to share yourself and invest what he has given to you in others with love, compassion, empathy and grace. Just remember this is a journey and no matter how much stress life throws at you, it most likely doesn't have to be solved tomorrow. Take the steps outlined in One Fish Changes Everything and overcome your challenges.

-Robert Holmes

ABOUT THE AUTHOR

Robert Holmes is a dynamic leader who started his business career as an entrepreneur his freshman year at Youngstown State University. Since then, he has started multiple small businesses. Most recently, he has served in the role of vice president of sales and marketing with a Fortune 500 company.

Robert is a dynamic speaker who feeds off the energy of his audience and can warm up the coldest room. He has engaged corporate audiences of 2,500 people, as well as small teams of ten.

His career has taught him that sometimes the best lessons learned through your successes, your ability to hit a number, or by addressing a large crowd. Sometimes they come from the most unexpected places. Robert currently lives on a small farm property in central Ohio with his wife of 19 years, Jen, and his sons Gavin and Rylan, three dogs, four chickens and a rabbit, who all contribute to his life's lessons. Every now and then he sends his friends an email, sharing lessons learned from a first-time chicken farmer and his belief that life's lessons can be found everywhere. You just have to be willing to recognize them.

www.leadershiplifecoach.com

It is with a sincere thank you that I'd like to invite you to visit my website at **www.onefishchanges.com** and download a simple file to help you and your planning. It will help you think through the needs of each step and I hope you find it helpful. Just always remember, the simpler the approach, the greater chance you have for success. Be patient, always learning, and know that *One Fish Changes Everything*.

"Required reading for anyone who wonders about their life purpose. *One Fish Changes Everything* is both thought-provoking and, in the end, an epiphany about finding joy in the everyday -- no matter your life stage, profession or economic status. Holmes's story is a modern day fable that shows the power of human kindness and the many truths just waiting to be discovered all around us."

Michele Kelly, *Today's Inspired Leader* and CEO, K+L
Storytellers

"Fishing for his dream fish may just land Joey the life of his dreams. *One Fish Changes Everything* is a heartfelt story with a powerful message that will keep you hooked page after page. You'll fall in love with the characters and find yourself searching for answers right alongside them. A wonderful debut novel from Robert Holmes."

Brittany Raschdorf, author of ***The Hypnotist's Daughter***

"*One Fish Changes Everything* is a MUST READ for anyone wants to grow as a leader, plus it is fun to read. Robert takes complex principles and ideas and makes them understandable and relatable through this great book."

Doug Garasic Author of ***Wayside*** Amazon #1 Selling Book + Pastor of Rustcity.Church

"I have had the pleasure to take the stage beside Robert addressing a few thousand people. His leadership, confidence and ability to relate to anyone is remarkable."

Jim Oberhofer Author of ***Top Fuel for Life, Speaker, Entrepreneur + Top Fuel Crew Chief***

"*One Fish Changes Everything* is a charming story about a student, a teacher and how life's greatest lessons are learned by having a plan, following a process, and making timely adjustments. Robert provides a simple framework for solving difficult challenges which will inspire his readers to, take control of their destiny and follow their dreams."

John Castelino, Vice President Global Marketing, Husband and Father of Two

"Robert Holmes is a proven leader whose experience shines through this delightful story that underscores the value of mentorship, simple life lessons, and the great past time of fishing. A worthy read that reminds us the most valuable lessons are often those learned along the way."

Harrison Rogers, Operations Executive

"Let me begin by saying I am amazed by the amount of character development accomplished in the first two chapters. I love the imagery. This book is perfect for anyone that has wanted something so badly it consumes every waking moment."

Katie Bischoff, Ohio Wesleyan Entrepreneurial Center

"Leadership lessons conveyed in a way that engages the mind, touches the heart and stirs the soul. Your life will be transformed as you apply this beautiful story to each sphere of your life. A read for anyone who wants to reach targets beyond the workplace and become a truly well-rounded leader."

Dave Jansen, Lead Pastor of CenterPointChurches.com

One Fish Changes Everything is a warm, compelling story that made me feel as though I was learning important life lessons right along with the characters. It was truly a joy to read, and Robert's descriptive words had me experiencing both the serenity and the excitement of being on the water as if I was there. It is a powerful message in a great book!

Dena Massaro-Williams, Cellist and Vocalist for Cirque du Soleil

ABOUT THE BOOK
ONE FISH CHANGES EVERYTHING

Joey Alfieri, his friends call him "Bags", finds himself in a unique situation. After some bad decisions and unfortunate luck, he is not moving forward in life and, quite frankly, isn't trying. The only thing he is passionate about is fishing, Oddly enough, a series of events leads him to uncover that an unlikely character can be his best chance of landing a giant. He sets on a journey that enables him to grasp a simple 4-step approach to reaching his goals, learn clear lessons of communicating with confidence, realize patience is a part of every strategic plan, soak up the importance of perspective and relationship in he does and recognizes that no matter how well you strategize you are never in complete control. Most important he realizes that One Fish Changes Everything!

My hope that you are inspired by this leadership book. Many lessons are learned throughout the book from all of those surrounding "Bags" and influencing in different ways. I hope that you pick up on the obvious lessons and the not so obvious ones that lead Bags to a place where he realizes that One Fish Changes Everything. Of all your choices, we hope you find this one of the best books to read.

EXCLUSIVE OFFER:
DOWNLOAD A FREE ONE FISH CHANGES EVERYTHING WORKBOOK

This workbook will enable you to re-visit some of the valuable lessons learned in the book. Use this workbook for a group study or to challenge yourself.

Father Defalco shared great Wisdom with Bags now make sure you get the most out of it as well.

Download on our website at: **www.onefishchanges.com**

If you enjoyed this book, I would greatly appreciate it if you would take a few minutes to provide a review on Amazon.com. Your reviews help others have an opportunity to read my book.

Made in the USA
Columbia, SC
23 January 2020